Praise for

MAKE OTHERS GREATER

"Gary Guller and Phillip Macko's engaging perspective on leadership and the importance of global diversity in the marketplace is as instructive as it is addictive. It will challenge your perspectives, it will inspire the way you lead, and it will do so in an incredibly entertaining way. It is a gem, expertly written and deeply insightful."

—V. R. Ferose
Senior Vice President, Globalization Services, SAP

"In *Make Others Greater*, Gary Guller and Phillip Macko successfully weave together lessons from a myriad of business books and publications, along with Gary's own true story. The book is both motivational and inspirational, taking business theories and combining them with Gary's real life adventure … and what an adventure it is! Even those who think they are familiar with Gary's story will gain a new perspective. His corporate speeches and talks reflect the same structure, but there is so much more to the story than anyone could ever imagine. The book shows the determination any major project can take, including the inevitable setbacks along the way. At the same time, it shows how the real point of any journey should be giving back, and helping mak

erating Officer
lutions Group

"They say it is all about perspective. Each obstacle or opportunity we encounter can be viewed from different perspectives. After meeting Gary, and surely after listening to what he has to say, yours will most likely change forever. My team and I met Gary in March 2013. When you lead a team, details matter. Nobody does a better job clarifying this point than Gary. Handing the youngest Sherpa chocolate every morning kept the engine of the team running. Not losing the focus despite challenges that are beyond our grasp rallied everybody on the team around a clear common goal. Finally, when your team meets a huge goal only to wake up the next morning ready and willing to face another challenge, you just know that you won. Gary is an inspiration. His humble, yet engaging way of sharing his story and insights will change your perspective forever. It will simply make you a better team player and a better leader."

—Nir Nimrodi, VP and General Manager
Animal & Food Safety at Life Technologies

"Although the book expertly details our expedition to base camp, there is so much more. *Make Others Greater* drives its powerful messages through real-world examples of expeditions, innovations and bold accomplishments balanced against folly, failure and hubris. Learning what to avoid as a leader is as important as knowing what to do – *Make Others Greater* provides insights into both. A must read!"

—Andy Cockrum
Documentary Filmmaker of *Team Everest: A Himalayan Journey*

"Gary Guller epitomizes the power of dreams and determination to overcome dangerous odds and deliver spectacular results. Operating from a higher consciousness of pure goodness, he achieved an incredible feat in climbing Mt. Everest with one arm. This fast-paced and enjoyable book shows how the lessons for leadership in sports and business are amazingly similar."

—Dr. Anil Maheshwari, Professor
Maharishi University of Management, Iowa

"When I first met Gary many years ago, he quoted Buddha: 'What we think, we become.' Gary has done just that. His story of persistence, teamwork, and the ability to overcome adversity is a lesson to us all. I am blessed to have played a small part in this incredible story."

—Janis P. Tupesis, MD FACEP FAAEM

"Gary and I traveled through Nepal for over a month, had great fun, faced death, and came back best friends. Gary has taught me and so many what it means to trust others, and best of all to 'stay focused and keep moving!' Gary Guller and Phillip Macko have brought to light Gary's historic summit of Mt. Everest and the internal journey of an extraordinary human being. If you or your organization are facing your own Everest, Gary's story will speak to you, move you, and give you the courage to keep moving forward."

—Marv Weidner, CEO
Managing Results, LLC

"Guller and Macko have magnificently captured the Voice of Greatness in leadership principles and core values. Gary's exploration stories will resonate with you until the very end. It is a must-read for everyone as it is life changing."

—Betty Garrett, CMP
President, Garrett Speakers International

"I first saw Gary speak seven years ago when he came to present to our company. Through his spoken words, his passion and unwavering dedication would stick with me for months following. That same experience emanates from the pages of his book. You won't put it down!"

—Mickey DiPietro, Head of Sales
Authentic8, Inc

"Mountain climber extraordinaire Gary Guller offers inspirational, down-to-earth tips on how to overcome adversity. Must reading!"

—David Heenan, Visiting Professor, Georgetown University
author, *Leaving On Top: Graceful Exits for Leaders*

"Gary Guller and Phillip Macko have combined forces to deliver a powerful and inspiring message in *Make Others Greater*. It's a book you'll find hard to put down, and a message you'll never forget."

—Madhu Hittuvalli, Chief Operations Officer
Dwise Soutions & Services Pvt. Limited, Bangalore, India

Make

Others

Greater

Make Others Greater™
From Mt. Everest to the Boardroom:
Vital Lessons from Dynamic Innovators, Explorers and Everyday Heroes
That Will Inspire the Way You Lead

Book design by Stacey Aaronson
www.creative-collaborations.com

Cover photos: Mt. Everest, Shackleton's *Endurance*, and Boardroom,
courtesy of Wikimedia Commons; Gary Guller, courtesy of author.

ISBN: 978-0-9888077-2-3

Published by:

Second Starters
San Diego, CA 92101

Second Starters is a registered trademark of Phillip Macko.

Printed in the USA

MAKE
OTHERS
GREATER

FROM MT. EVEREST
TO THE BOARDROOM:

VITAL LESSONS *from* DYNAMIC
INNOVATORS, EXPLORERS *and*
EVERYDAY HEROES THAT WILL
INSPIRE *the* WAY YOU LEAD

GARY GULLER & PHILLIP MACKO

Second Starters®

Along the Journey's Path

In the early days it was our family who taught us how to be, how to share, how to grow.

Then it was our childhood friends who taught us how to play, how to compete, and how to win or lose.

When we crossed into adulthood and into the pursuit of our lives' missions, once divergent but now converging, it was our colleagues and mentors who taught us how to dream, how to set goals, and how to be part of a team.

Eventually we started families of our own who taught us how to be humble, how to forgive, and how to truly love.

Along the way upward we've loved and lost; we've shared and grown. We've tried and failed; we've dusted ourselves off and tried again. And at crucial moments we beat the odds, quieted the critics and naysayers, and celebrated our victories.

Through it all, you were all a part of our journey and we dedicate our book to you.

Gary Guller and Phillip Macko

MEETING GARY GULLER

Meeting Gary Guller is like referring to an edition of the dictionary that didn't print the word *impossible*. We refer to dictionaries not for knowledge but for meanings to words that we find hard to understand. When you hear Gary speak as you sit in the audience, or when you have a one-on-one chat with him, he answers many of your questions before you even ask them.

Gary Guller is the first person with one arm to summit Mount Everest. He also led the world's largest-ever cross-disability group to the Everest Base Camp. And this did not happen easily, for beyond the physical effort it takes to climb Everest, there is also a long road of preparation.

Imagine what it takes to bring a large group of people with cross-disabilities together to achieve what most people (without any disabilities) only dream about. It takes much more than training and funds; it takes a vision beyond oneself.

When he says: "Thirty five years of passion, focus, and dedication for thirty-one minutes on the top of the world," it covers a lot. Rework that sentence in your mind and it explodes into thousands of pieces, each answering many questions in your life about passion, work, ambition, wants, desire, teamwork, commitment, trust, and more. It even tells you about the unpredictability of life and the balance that you keep as you walk through it, and above all the importance of every moment you live in.

Just before the talk, when we shared a few minutes together and got introduced, an interesting fact struck me. Gary as a motivational speaker often communicates with many CEOs and top executives who head organizations and groups in the corporate world, and the reason they look to Gary for inspiration is likely because he has literally been on top of the world. In their journeys to the top of their organizations, who else can be a better inspiration and coach than Gary?

I have heard several motivational speakers in my life, but not many times do you get to see someone who doesn't quote from others' lives but tells his own story and it inspires you.

When Gary tells you what he did, you will be inspired ... when you read this book, you'll be inspired. And it will change you. You'll be better because of it.

—Vinod Narayan

CONTENTS

Summit Day: Mt. Everest, 5/23/2003

HORSESHOES

Survival alone doesn't define us. It's what we learn from the experience that does.

We stumble. We fall. We risk. We fail.

We rise again.

We innovate. We persevere. We inspire. We conquer.

Such is the human condition. We choose between two paths in each interconnected moment. One path leads upward, forever upward. The other leads to ambivalence, eventually to mediocrity, then to irrelevance.

Most of us will never summit Mt. Everest. We'll not endure the blurry fog of oxygen deprivation in a place holding the ultimate consequence as reward for a misstep.

We'll not dig our crampons into the base of Hillary Step, with full knowledge that death awaits below us. We'll not have the realization that those before us who successfully navigated The Step and summited had the benefit of using two hands to secure themselves with, that an already technically difficult climb becomes highly improbable when facing it with only one arm.

We'll not make an unimaginable sacrifice of ourselves. We'll not watch others in our journey pass away before us or next to us as a direct consequence of the quest.

But we all climb our own Everest.

The toughest problems we've faced and overcome define our capacity of strength. They represent the "edge" – a place we know we can take ourselves without fear of falling hopelessly over.

If our roles never required us to go beyond the "known edge," this book may be just an interesting and entertaining adventure read.

It's intended to be much more.

The story of Gary Guller is inspiring and empowering. It's flawed and imperfect. It's full of feats and of follies, of passions and of addictions. In its narrative we learn to lift up others, and to rise up within ourselves. We understand the simple beauty of core vision and the danger of straying too far from it. We face the measure of ultimate sacrifice, and we understand the human effect of overcoming it.

And more.

Together, we'll set sail with Sir Ernest Shackleton. We'll sit in the boardrooms of two companies and learn why one is gone and the other thrives. We'll reflect on the simple yet beautifully diverse message of the Sherpa and take their wisdom with us as we face the day tomorrow. We'll discover lost Renaissance art and apply our knowledge to how we see others around us.

Two years ago, quite by chance, I sat next to a man in a Washington DC bar who would help to change the course of my life. His name was Andy Cockrum, and he was the documentarian who filmed *Team Everest: A Himalayan Journey* – the film that chronicled the '03 expedition that Gary led.

Months later I was introduced to Gary. By our second conversation, I felt like Bilbo Baggins on the day he first joined forces with Gandalf.

We live in a world where the sensationally bad story opens the nightly news, and the story of hope is relegated to lesser prominence. Where the Kardashians and Lindsay Lohan are household names.

As Bilbo, I would champion the cause of raising awareness about something nobler. I would bring this incredible story of ability to a world I felt needed to hear it.

It resonated with me first at a personal level. Sixteen years ago I lost two brothers, Steven and Eddie. They were playing horseshoes in the backyard together on the day of Steven's wedding when the same bolt of lightning struck them both. Tragically, a day of celebration turned to one of unimaginable loss when the lightning claimed their lives.

Like Gary, our family rose up beyond the loss.

When I returned home from the hospital after a traumatic amputation of my left index finger, I planned to wear a black glove over my left hand to disguise what I saw as a hideous disfigurement. Today I don't wear that glove.

Gary once concealed his missing left arm by tucking the sleeve of his shirt into a jacket, one he wore in extreme heat as well as cold. Today he wears Hawaiian print shirts.

I personally related to Gary on so many levels. So do countless others. All who meet him, who attend his presentations, who hear about his exploits – they all relate.

That is perhaps the greatest pull of his story.

We're CEOs. We're moms and dads. We're influencers and change agents. We're future leaders. We're all people whose lives are important, and who intersect with and influence the paths of others.

Individually, we face the common foes of change and adversity. It's a battle we face alone, but a path we share with all others. We each climb our own Everest in the challenges we rise up against and overcome.

As Gary and I explored the possibilities of our "Gandalf's quest" together, we soon realized that the stories transcended personal into professional. Gary being an internationally known inspirational speaker and corporate trainer, my being an executive in music publishing with international training and consulting experience.

It was a natural progression from home to work and we followed it.

Disability is the limitation we place on ourselves.

Leaders inspire others to reach greater heights, to push past self-imposed limitations. They make heroes of those around them by inspiring others to accomplish more than they individually believed possible.

We're all leaders in our own way, whether titled so or informally appointed, and to be a leader is to make others greater along the way – to have the belief that any willing person can go beyond the accomplishments of today, and to never abandon that belief.

Leadership is about moving forward and forever upward, regardless of the magnitude of setback experienced along the way.

Phillip Macko
April 7, 2013

ONE

THE NEW RESILIENCE

MAKE

Every action impacts the team

OTHERS

Sacrifice is a key ingredient in the success recipe

GREATER

The unbridled pursuit of more is dangerous

People ask me, 'What is the use of climbing Mount Everest?' and my answer must at once be, 'It is of no use. There is not the slightest prospect of any gain whatsoever. Oh, we may learn a little about the behavior of the human body at high altitudes, and possibly medical men may turn our observation to some account for the purposes of aviation. But otherwise nothing will come of it. We shall not bring back a single bit of gold or silver, not a gem, nor any coal or iron … If you cannot understand that there is something in man which responds to the challenge of this mountain and goes out to meet it, that the struggle is the struggle of life itself upward and forever upward, then you won't see why we go. What we get from this adventure is just sheer joy. And joy is, after all, the end of life. We do not live to eat and make money. We eat and make money to be able to live. That is what life means and what life is for.'

—George Mallory,
Climbing Everest: The Complete Writings of George Mallory

ORIZABA

"Too damned fast. We're falling too damn fast.
        No choice now. We will stop.
        And I will die."

Moments before, his teammate had lost his footing. The sound of him yelling "falling!" rang simultaneous to the force of his weight on the climbing rope the team shared. It first compromised the hold of Gary, then Jerry Webster. They were sprung into a weightless free fall down the mountainside.

In a desperate effort to break the screaming plummet of their bodies, Gary twisted mid-air and thrust his foot forward in an attempt to imbed his crampon into the ice.

The ice was unwelcoming. The fall continued.

He swung his ice axe towards the slope. The slope rejected it, propelling it backward and hard into his right eyebrow.

He swung again, this time finding purchase. His crampons took hold, but the collective weight of his teammates tore him away yet again.

It happened too fast for him to register that his left wrist was still tethered. His ice axe stubbornly held fast to the mountain, and for several long moments it refused to relinquish its hold on Gary's left arm. In violent protest it gave a greedy yank that ripped the nerves controlling his left arm from his spinal cord before releasing its hold on Gary as he began again to drop.

The fall came much faster now. The boulders below rushed to meet the climbers at speeds exceeding forty miles per hour.

Then the fall reached its unavoidable end, and for a moment there was only darkness.

He revived to the taste of blood and the feel of it dripping down his face.

He heard his best friend Jerry scream for him. Jerry was ten feet away, battered and bleeding. His other mate's body lay thirty feet further down the mountain, bent unnaturally over a boulder.

He urgently took inventory of his capabilities, noting an intense throbbing in his ankle and right hand. There was no feeling in his left arm. He was unable to stand.

Jerry and Gary attempted to force themselves down the mountain toward their friend in an effort to reunite the team. Their movements set off a cascade of rocks. A boulder slammed hard into Jerry's head. He screamed out, the shrill of his voice testifying to the severity of the insult to his body.

They were forced to abandon the effort to reach their friend. Instead they surrendered to the cold night air, and to the inevitability that they may not survive.

It was decided that neither would let the other go unaccompanied on the final journey they braced themselves for. With that they both closed their eyes.

In the morning Jerry lay three feet from Gary. He'd gone on to break the deal, to transition alone. Jerry's lifeless body was free of the pain and suffering he'd endured the night before.

The remaining two climbers reeled from the loss and braced themselves to survive another day. Backpacks with water and other provisions were long lost in the fall. They were left to face the day's glaring high-altitude sunlight with no means to quench their thirst, to face the brutal, bitter cold of night without the benefit of shelter.

They would wait there another day before rescue would arrive, and an additional day before their rescuers could safely evacuate them from the mountain.

Their rescuers would arrive with only body bags. They didn't expect to find survivors.

This is the beginning of a story that would change the course of an untold number of people's lives.

Imagine for a moment that you were in their place. What thoughts would fly through your mind as you braced against each moment, wondering if rescue would arrive in time, or if frostbite and injury would ultimately win the battle they were waging on your life?

Whatever fleeting thoughts may have been running at sprint-speed through Gary's mind, one theme would bind them all together into a single urgent purpose.

Survival.

It's this stubborn refusal to surrender that defines resilience. And it's a new kind of resilience that defines leadership in the New Normal.

BY WAY OF THE DODO

William H. Russell knew he was onto something.

He had the competitive advantage he needed to become the go-to communications solution of the day. He'd built a system that could cut the time it took to deliver mail by as much as 60%.

He quickly needed to staff up his company, so he ran the following ad: "Wanted: Young, skinny, wiry fellows not over 18. Must be expert riders, willing to risk death daily. Orphans preferred. Wages: $25 per week."

Applicants swarmed the company's way stations that were placed approximately fifteen miles apart, spanning the distance between Missouri and California.

Though it wasn't cheap, the Pony Express was the expedient answer to getting important mail across the country faster.

By stagecoach it took twenty-four days from door to door, Missouri to Sacramento. In 1860, The Pony Express did it in seven-and-a-half days.

Russell had cornered the market, but only for just over a year. In 1861 the transcontinental telegraph was completed and on October 26, 1861, the Pony Express closed its doors.[1]

The year prior, another budding entrepreneur put his novel idea to the test. John Wise believed that ground travel severely constrained the delivery of mail. He would take to the air instead.

On August 17, 1859, the hot air balloon Jupiter took to the skies. It departed Lafayette, Indiana, with 123 letters destined for New York City.

A stiff wind blew it south once it reached the necessary 14,000 feet in elevation. Five hours later, having traveled only thirty miles, it reached Crawfordsville, Indiana. There Mr. Wise gave all 123 letters to the nearest postal agent he could find, who put them on the next train bound for NYC.

Ninety-four years later, the last letter was sent through the pneumatic tubes hidden under the streets of New York City. The "racketeers" who fed the tubes had been responsible for delivering nearly 55% of the city's mail at one time. But no longer.

Though the tubes shot mail across the city at speeds reaching one hundred miles per hour, they were grossly inefficient and highly expensive to use. Nothing weighing more than five pounds could ever be sent through them, only one piece of mail could be placed in the system every twelve seconds, and all pieces within the tubes at any given time had to be of the exact same dimensions.

The system was permanently abandoned in 1953. Remnants of it can still be found under the city.

Throughout time the need for rapid, adaptive change has been recognized – by some.

And completely missed by others.

DOMINO

From 1950 through the end of 1999, the US economy grew at a steady and predictable pace. From 2000–2007 that pace would slow to an average of 2%. During the fourth quarter of 2007, the first warning sign of things to come would arrive when growth slowed considerably – to below 0.7%.

What followed next was an economic free fall rivaling the severity and suddenness of the one experienced at Orizaba. In what's widely considered to be the worst economic collapse since the Great Depression, institutions lined up like dominos…

… And fell – one into the next.

The total collapse of the financial sector led to major banks requiring bailouts in order to merely survive. Stock markets around the world contracted and refused to rebound. The housing market imploded, followed by an exponential rise in loan defaults, evictions, and foreclosure.

The dominos next fell across companies, causing an estimated 200,000 small businesses to close, along with major national retailers such as Circuit City. Moving beyond to the private sector, declines in consumer wealth occurred in the trillions.

The world stage was set in a similar fashion as some economies teetered precariously close to the edge, while others emerged as new market leaders.

For the next four years, the world fell into global recession. Eventually, the last domino dropped and the New Normal began.

During the Depression era, the US experienced a shift in its economic base from agricultural to industrial. In the 1980s another shift occurred, moving the US economy from an industrial to a service-oriented base. The New Normal has brought with it yet another shift, one whose destination is not completely clear.

One thing *is* clear, however; the paradigms of the past have been shattered. In October, 1998, Peter Drucker[2] warned that our assumptions on business, technology, and organizations were based in large part on fifty-year-old theory. He strongly warned that few policies – and few assumptions about the economy, business, or technology – remain true for even twenty or thirty years.

If he were alive today, Mr. Drucker would say that those increments have contracted to single years, even months and weeks.

The New Normal necessitates a new level of nimbleness.

SURAJ

After the fall Gary was told by his neurosurgeon that he'd never regain the use of his left arm. He tried experimental surgery but was left in excruciating pain, rather than seeing the improvement he'd hoped for.

In 1989, three years post-Orizaba, he made an unimaginable decision. He asked his doctors to amputate his left arm.

His brother Richard described the recovery period post-amputation as a time Gary's family lost him to an obsession. The countless hours Gary spent in the gym in an effort to regain his strength and athleticism left no doubt as to his intentions.

He would climb again.

Once ready, Gary ventured back to the world he knew and loved, one he'd very nearly lost. He started slowly, camping and hiking across Canada and the western US. It didn't take long for his appetite for more to grow insatiable. Soon he was crossing the sea to explore the mountains of Wales and experience ice climbing in Scotland.

He first visited Nepal, Tibet, and China in the '90s. Not long after he was leading expeditions there. In 1997 he signed on to a friend's expedition to climb Lhotse, a peak adjoining Everest.

Arun Treks and Expeditions USA was born, beginning first in his mind, and later in reality. It would be a tribute to his fallen friends, Jerry Webster and Mal Duff (who'd died in his sleep at base camp). It would be part of the journey to his eventual goal: to climb Mt. Everest.

Face the setback. Recommit and rebuild. The Suraj will rise again.

DOORS

They will dream sometime, and when they dream about this area
(Everest) they will be happy for a few days.
Because wherever you go, it comes in dream.

—Nima Dawa Sherpa, April 6, 2003

Four years later, Gary arrived at a hotel in El Paso, Texas, wrestling with himself to find the words he needed. As he looked at the attendees of the convention where he'd been invited to speak, he struggled with the notion that he was somehow different from them. He urgently looked within for a way to strike common ground with the group, as a speaker must.

Leading up to this moment, Gary knew only a handful of people with disabilities. Though his arm had been lost years before, he felt at first disconnected and foreign to the group he prepared to address. He thought long and hard, and he came to the realization that he was no different from the attendees.

He was, in fact, one with them.

Up to that moment, Gary had yet to reconcile himself with the emotional and physical aspects of the loss of his arm. Both would greet him onstage as he stepped forward to the microphone and spoke the first words of his presentation to his newly acknowledged brothers and sisters: the members of the Coalition of Texans with Disabilities.

Director Dennis Borel described the applause that Gary received on completion of his talk as thunderous. All fell silent when a wheelchair-bound attendee of the convention asked Gary to take him up the mountain with him next time.

Hours later, awaiting his return flight while having beers with Dennis, Gary decided he liked the idea. On the flight home it played like a movie in his head. TE '03, The Team Everest expedition was soon born.

So many things had to be considered in the days before Gary accepted the role of expedition leader to Team Everest '03 (TE '03).

Gary is an extreme athlete. His adrenaline begins when others decide it better to turn around and go back.

I'll take them to the edge, knowing I'm just getting started, he thought.

It's easy to say yes to something half a world away when you're in Austin, Texas, with running water, electricity, and cars … with family and friends. Many had come and gone before those who volunteered to be a part of TE '03 – all with the intention to reach Everest base camp or further.

"When they say they want to go to Everest with me, I think to myself: *You haven't even begun to comprehend what you're going to give up in order to follow through with that commitment.*"

The TE '03 volunteers are different. They're committed. They understand loss. Overcoming it is their daily experience.

The team is formed shorty after. It consists of an Army vet in a wheelchair; a twenty-something Sri Lankan immigrant with one leg; a WalMart tire manager left paraplegic by a motorcycle wreck; a middle-aged man set on world travel despite being unable to move anything below his neck; a deaf teacher; two Nepali Sherpa amputees considered karma-cursed by their countrymen; a US Navy vet enduring debilitating pain from her Gulf War injury; and an overweight, bipolar divorcee with fibromyalgia.

With the team in place, other priorities present themselves. The first is how to finance the trip. The idea is becoming a reality, now the money must follow.

Gary knocks on doors, something like 300 of them. Some see his proposal as a scam, nothing more than a publicity stunt. The Ardoin family, and soon 1,500 others understand it at a deeper level.

Now the real work begins.

FLAWS

In the early 2000s Toyota sat atop the throne, leading the field as the top automotive manufacturer worldwide. Fast forward to 2009, and a far different view of the company emerges, one seeing the giant brought nearly to its knees by massive recalls and plummeting stock prices.

At the pinnacle of its problem years, Toyota had to reconcile itself with certain realities. It faced recalls exceeding 14 million due to unintended acceleration issues.[3] Its consumer base in China (previously the largest of its territories) eroded by nearly 50% due to rising political tensions between China and Japan. It faced major interruptions to its supply chain due to the tsunami of 2010.

Toyota was in crisis.

Up to this point they'd shrugged off the recall, claiming driver error amongst other explanations as the cause of the vehicle acceleration issues. With consumer confidence rapidly eroding, they opted to take a different approach. President Aoki Toyoda stepped forward with an apology to its consumer base, and in doing so admitted that the company had problems, that it had grown too big, too fast.

He explained that his company had lost touch with its customer, and lost control of its quality. Plants that once prided themselves on worker accuracy had given way to worker complacency amidst the crushing demand created by Toyota's too rapid world expansion.

The once dominant car manufacturer exposed its flaws openly to the world. This remarkably brave admission stood in contrast to its country's centuries-old practices.

Its workers took notice.

They soon embraced a nobler cause. They would once again become a proud and leading organization. Their company's name would again be synonymous with quality.

Toyota's willingness to acknowledge its errors and overhaul its product development has inspired confidence in its shareholders and a renewed sense of purpose in its workforce.

It's time to embrace openness. Word, both good and bad, travels fast.

Let the word come from you first.

The time has passed for playing corporate hide-and-seek.

It's simply no longer possible.

To one degree or another, most businesses have embraced the idea of transparency. We live in a fast-moving, flattened fishbowl world. Social Media, Smartphones, and other advances have seen to that. Businesses understand that their customers are talking about them in these ever-developing social spaces; they're learning that it's good to listen. And to talk back.

Rand Fishkin, CEO of SEOmoz, has taken corporate communication and brand interaction to brave new levels – into the deep, deep waters of translucence.

If you look on the company website, you'll see their funding decks. You'll read about both their successes and their failures.

If you read Mr. Fishkin's personal blog, you'll see a copy of his last performance review.

Unedited. Un-doctored. Honest. Real.

I'm starting the really slow clapping that we all know (from movies) builds into a crescendo.

It's applause directed at you, Rand. Well done.

Reinvention begins with brutally honest self-reflection. The evolution next leads to open, honest dialogue, then to committed change.

To understand weakness in this way is to gain strength, but to ignore weakness is to begin the slow march that inevitably leads to a corporate graveyard.

SIXTH PLACE

Houston Natural Gas and InterNorth merged to become a single corporation in 1985. The new company's name will never be forgotten.

Enron.

Trace the Enron story back to the zero point: Boil down their complex opera of errors, and the first key ingredient in their recipe for collapse comes clearly into view: their failure to admit to and address problems in their earliest (and most manageable) stages.

In Enron's case, the company wasn't reaching the aggressive financial targets set before it. Their problem required that a new foundation for the company be poured. Their eventual solution was to throw a roll of duct tape into the basement. Their tactics were prime contributors to what became the sixth largest corporate bankruptcy in US history.

In the early days, Enron did well. Legitimately. It acquired a team of market speculators who made the company a great deal of money. This initial success lent credibility to the Enron name and made them a Wall Street favorite. Enron also benefited at this time from the fiscally responsible leadership of Rich Kinder (from 1990 to 1996), who ran the company based on conservative accounting best practices.

Although the speculators – now called traders – began practicing sleight of hand to meet and exceed year-over-year results, they were kept at bay by Mr. Kinder.

But only for a time.

For reasons unrelated to business, Kinder left the organization in 1996, and so began the reign of Jeffrey Skilling. Soon after, Enron forever lost its moral compass.

David Copperfield might have been impressed with the speculator's newly found "art of illusion" prowess under Skilling – that is, if the speculator's financial prestidigitation hadn't (for example) eventually caused massive power outages in and unbelievable debt for the State of California.

When income from the trader's activities began to produce losses, Jeffrey Skilling's out-of-control utilization of mark-to-market accounting was Enron's answer. Skilling's changes to the way losses were reported by the company were combined with Andy Fastow's unbridled financial shell games, ones in which he used a spiderweb of interconnected dumping-ground corporations to mask a financial toothache that eventually grew to a full-mouth festering abscess.

Skilling and Fastow played similar games with assets and properties under the Enron umbrella. Mark-to-market accounting (something Skilling required as a condition of his promotion) allowed Enron to book future "anticipated" revenues as today's actual income, even when the property's income it was applied to had yet to be realized.

Mark-to-market, it should be noted, is common in securities but dangerous when applied to other business models. Enron was active in other business models. Thayer Watkins of San Jose State University provides the following example[4]:

A power plant is built costing $4 million. It has an expected after-interest yield of $9.9 million across its ten-year expected lifetime. Profits are therefore projected to be $5.9 million. Under mark-to-market, this $5.9 million profit is booked at the time the power plant is completed, though it hasn't produced "dollar-one" in real revenue. There's only "anticipated" income.

It's not hard to substantiate profit projections when you're measuring them against future projections that you're making up. Literally making up.

We all know how this story ends.

CITIES

Other companies make better choices when the numbers aren't aligning – ones grounded in intellect and innovation.

Few better examples of corporate resilience exist than IBM's successful reinvention. Once the world's leading provider of large mainframe computers, it's shifted its focus to providing eloquent high-tech, data-driven solutions.

When the rise in personal computing, driven by Silicon Valley, and the revolution in client/server technologies threatened IBM's core model, it set out on a bold and necessary new course. Now the employer to 400,000 is positioned to significantly impact system-wide improvements in healthcare, transportation, energy, public safety, water, and educational systems in keeping with its Smarter Planet/Smarter Cities models.

It traded its hardware-centric model for one driven by smart analytics and data. In doing so, IBM helped improve efficiencies throughout the world through its data-centric, consultative approach to problem solving.

As IBM will attest, reinvention often demands loss before it allows gain. It requires a step backward before it allows the many steps forward that will follow.

Personal reinvention demands the same.

AGILIENCE

In the time between watching the *Team Everest: A Himalayan Journey* documentary and beginning to write this book, I came across a story of Gary as a teenage boy in an archived newspaper article. I'd been moved by it, and it became my first choice of perspectives for the next chapter.

It read as perfectly as a Hollywood scriptwriter could pen it. The teenage Gary holds a picture of Everest in his hand and knows with certainty, in that adolescent moment, that he will one day conquer it. As moving a story as it was to tell, I was glad when Gary told me that this wasn't at all how it actually happened.

He did remember the day he first saw that picture, and he recalled that he hadn't a clue that he'd one day summit Everest (though he knew he'd see it). In his words: "I didn't know what the hell I was gonna do; I just knew that whatever it was, it was gonna be big."

It was the evolution of Gary's dream, one that began in his early teens, that would change the lives of so many.

In an ever-changing world, the notion of predestined certainty is a fleeting one – the stuff of romanticized movies and puffed-up peddlers of gooey positivity at best.

In the past, resilience was largely a function of optimistic reactivity. When something unexpected happened, we braced ourselves for the predictable outcome. We knew that the war would end, the economy would rebound from recession, and our lost job would eventually be replaced by our next opportunity.

We don't know these things with any degree of certainty anymore in the New Normal.

"Today's world is an interconnected, interdependent, diverse, unpredictable, and unstable global community," says Douglas

LaBier, PhD, in his brilliant article "The New Resilience."[5] LaBier suggests that our current understanding of resiliency is a "rearview mirror" one. We believe that we can still bounce back by learning from past mistakes and correcting our paths in a way that allows us to return to stability and balance. "You can't re-establish equilibrium in a constantly shifting world," he says.

The new view is *agilience* – or agile resilience. To adopt agilience is to understand that technology has collapsed the timeframes we once applied to progress. Our world therefore evolves away from what we knew at record speeds, and will evolve more quickly toward a future that will again change. Stability and balance are a thing of the past, temporary at best in the comfort they offer. Forward movement and shifting paradigms are the waypoints of the New Normal.

Agilience doesn't demand that you know where you're going, because you can't always know. It doesn't require that you have all the answers; the answers of yesterday often don't apply today.

To be agilient simply means you're committed to continue upward. Whatever setback or loss (Gary), whatever change in market conditions or technologies (IBM) may come, you'll survive, adapt, and eventually overcome.

Most of all, it requires a vision for the future that is understanding of, but non-reliant on, the past.

TWO

Make Others Greater

MAKE

Seek out and build upon common ground

OTHERS

Lift up and celebrate others

GREATER

Fuel the desire in others to be a part of something that is bigger than themselves

For Lakpa Sherpa it was a great honor for him to see something he'd only heard of – to see this Living Goddess. Every day when we got to camp, even when he couldn't see Everest, he would sit and pray toward Everest. Every time we would cross a bridge, he'd throw flowers for blessings for this expedition. Every time the sun came up, he'd pray for this expedition.

—Gary Guller, *Team Everest: A Himalayan Adventure*

ONLY ONE PER MEAL

In 1999 Ken Ahroni was enjoying the family Thanksgiving feast. As the tryptophan began to take effect from the several helpings of turkey he'd eaten, he made a semi-drowsy and quite random observation.

Every Thanksgiving there was usually only one wishbone.

Many may have made a similar observation at least once in their lifetime. Most have dismissed it. Only Ken went on to create a million-dollar business because of it.

Lucky Break® manufactures synthetic wishbones that have both the sound and the tactile feel of a real turkey wishbone. Their daily production run averages 30,000. Their product offering has even expanded to include custom-designed, imprinted wishbones for corporate and promotional use. Their story has appeared in *Inc., Fortune Small Business, Country Living,* and *Entrepreneur.*

The difference between a brilliant idea and absolute folly is mostly this: commitment.

VOICES

It starts with a single drop of water. You follow its trail downward until it reaches a theater stage below where the conductor stands. It moves through him, and then at once is dispersed in a wave of energy across the floor. The movement of the now-electrified water imitates the dance of aquatic creatures under a luminescent bay. When the visualized energy reaches the back of the stage, it begins its climb upward. It illuminates row upon row of video monitors.

In each, a face. And from each face, a voice.

Eric Whitacre is a composer of classic music. One day a friend stumbled on a YouTube video that had been posted by Britlin Losee for him. It was of her singing the soprano part to one of his compositions.

That's simply how it began.

An idea formed, and he pursued it. He blogged regularly, each entry explaining his vision. He hoped to gather together fifty participants to join his Virtual Choir. He created a dedicated YouTube channel and Google Hangouts where he posted singing lessons. He recorded himself conducting the movements and voices that would combine to create the visualization of his song. He asked those who wished to join his virtual choir to record themselves singing a voice to one of his selected compositions.

That was then.

This is now, and Eric's third Virtual Choir video is called "Water Night." It contains 3,746 individual videos, all singing in one of six choral voices. Contributors represent 73 different countries.

For most of his life, another man had wanted to express himself vocally in a choir along with others. Being legally blind prevented him from joining, as he could never get close enough to see the conductor's prompting.

Now he sits directly in front of his computer screen. Now he's one voice among the many that together are the Virtual Choir.[6]

THE WILD, WOBBLY WHEELS

In 1953 Sir Edmund Hillary and Sherpa Tenzing Norgay became the first to reach the peak of Mt. Everest. On the 50th anniversary of Hillary and Norgay's successful summit, a new breed of climbers began their own record-setting adventure.

They gathered together at the Austin, Texas, airport to begin their grueling journey across the world. The flight to Los Angeles was uneventful. It offered a false sense of comfort that the remainder of the journey would betray.

After arriving at LAX, team member Dinesh Rasinghe fell when his daypack rubbed against his new prosthetic. Mastery of movement with his new leg, built specifically for the rigors of the trail, would require practice and patience in order for him to move with the necessary cadence.

Mark Ezell watched with concern as the front wheels of his new titanium chair wobbled wildly, causing him to doubt its ability to guide him through the airport corridors. He opted to ride on a luggage cart instead. Mark wondered if the wheels could survive the unpredictable terrain of the trail if they couldn't even negotiate a paved airport hallway.

Riley Woods accepted the help of a stranger offering him assistance while boarding the plane in Taipei. He watched in disbelief as the stranger flung Riley's chair and backpack over his shoulder and quickly disappeared. Riley would arrive in Bangkok hours later to find his chair waiting for him. His backpack, full of medicine, money, and other vital supplies was long gone.

Thirty-six hours from Austin they arrived safely in Kathmandu, Nepal. The realization that the trip was indeed happening washed across the weary travelers, as did the knowledge that the hardships they faced in getting there were minor in comparison to the ones that the Everest trail would offer.

This fact merely fixed their resolve to go further onward, and inevitably upward. They had faith and belief in themselves.

And in their leader.

DUX DUCIS

In 1987 authors Jim Kouzes and Barry Posner wrote the landmark, evidence-based book *The Leadership Challenge*.[7] It's now in its fifth edition and just celebrated its 25th anniversary.

In its first edition, surveys conducted found that 62% of employees admired leaders who were "forward looking." As of the fifth edition, published in 2012, that number rose to 71%. Additionally, 58% of employees in 1987 wanted to work with leaders who were inspiring. As of the fifth edition, that number has risen to 70%.

Of all the important takeaways the book offers, one message resonated: Leaders must be inspired by a vision beyond their own. "It's not just the leader's vision that's important. It has to be a shared vision."[8]

Such was the construct that Sam Wurtzel used to build his first stores in the early 1950s. Following the end of the Second World War, there were 12 million Americans in uniform, destined to return home. This would mark the start of a ten-plus year baby boom.

It was the perfect time to be in the TV and appliance business.

Soon, Wards TV was born, and over the coming years it grew to become a nationwide chain of 500 stores posting billions in annual sales.

And then it fell.

Sam was an audacious thinker, his ideas described as recklessly intrepid. When it came to core values, the "One Face Policy" stood above all others: espousing fair and honest dealings with customers, staff, and suppliers. Sam believed in the value of creating a fully transparent environment of autonomy that was risk friendly, not risk adverse.

He carefully built his organization on the foundation of quality personnel. Each new hire was screened using a battery of tests developed by industrial psychologists to ensure the candidate possessed both the skills and personality traits necessary to thrive in their corporate culture. Once hired, each became an integral part of the company who bought into and vested in the company's vision of transparency, innovation, and integrity.

Wards' revenue grew exponentially between years 1963 and 1970, moving the needle from approximately $8 million to over $61 million in seven short years.

But cracks began to develop in the glass slippers of this Cinderella story as Wards TV took on its new persona.

In Good to Great to Gone: The Sixty Year Rise and Fall of Circuit City,[9] the author carefully chronicles the early rise and eventual fall of the retail giant from a unique and intimate perspective: that of former CEO, founder of Circuit City and son of Ward's original founder Sam Wurtzel.[10]

Author Alan Wurtzel held the top position at Circuit City from 1973 to 1986 and remained on the board until 2001. He played an active role in the early days of the transition from Wards TV to Circuit City prior to his departure.

Years before becoming Circuit City, and even more years before its fall, Wards TV had amassed impressive revenues. Its sales and management teams were comprised of well-trained professionals. It was poised for greatness.

But there were also shortcomings.

In his forthright manner, author Alan Wurtzel points to a critical flaw in the organization's discipline to the strategic planning process as an early challenge the company had to overcome.

He describes the budget-development process as one that occurred on the "back of an envelope," a process very different from the meticulous and specific one used to track and monitor expenses, or the great care with which staff was selected, trained, and promoted.

The "back of the envelope" held little effort to budget sales, gross margins, or merchandise categories. Nor did it attempt to anticipate changes in product mix and margins.

Vision and transparency combined with inspired leadership can't fill the organizational void left by inadequate strategic planning.

In the section titled The Undisciplined Pursuit of More, Alan Wurtzel references a telling quote from then-partner and board member A.L. Hecht.[11] "We are like the universe. We never stop expanding." The gargantuan growth of Wards to Circuit City, and Circuit City across the nation, would play an integral role in its demise.

Venturing too far beyond the core focus of the mission creates a splintered effort and exposes opportunities for compounding errors. It tugs at the leadership's core vision, sometimes leading it too far astray.

LIFTING UP SHANNON

The dream that drove Babu Chiri Sherpa was not to climb the mountain the fastest, though he did. It was not to spend the most time on the mountain without oxygen, nor was it to ascend the mountain ten times – although he did both. His dream was of a better life for his six daughters, of them having the freedom to choose the life they wanted.

He began his relationship with the mountain as a porter at age thirteen. He taught himself to read and write because he lacked the opportunity to learn through formal education.

He climbed in the hopes of generating sponsorships for the $11,000 he needed to build a five-room school in his village of Akang, a place where his daughters could receive the formal education he never had – a place that would allow his daughters to have choices beyond the shadow of the mountain.

In April 2001, during what would have been his eleventh summit, he lost his footing and fell. His body was recovered a day later. In Nepal, at base camp, a stone memorial (chorten) was built in honor of the man many believe to be one of the greatest Everest climbers.

Just two years later, Gary and his team placed the last stone on top of a four-foot monument near Babu Sherpa's. It was built in honor of another fallen hero. Her name was Shannon Ardoin.

Though her feet never touched the mountainside, her spirit touched each climber on the Team Everest '03 expedition and everyone who knew her during her short but special life. Her story would embody the core vision of Gary Guller and the mission of the Team Everest '03 expedition.

Shannon lived with her family in Flower Mound, Texas. It was a compromised life; she was born with a brain condition that prevented her from seeing, speaking, and even moving.

It would have been very easy for the family to institutionalize Shannon, or place her in foster care. Her family instead chose to give Shannon the life she was born into, that of being a cherished member of the Ardoin family.

And so she was.

Shannon became one of the most popular students at her local high school. She was once presented with Homecoming flowers by a group of her school's football players. They always visited Shannon before the game and shared their victories and defeats with her afterwards.

Ken and Annette Ardoin provided Gary with two of their daughter's belongings to take with him on the journey in memory of her passing: a lacy sampler with her name cross-stitched in pink (that was given to her at birth), and a rosary from her godmother, made from pressed rose petals and blessed by the Pope.

At the crest of a hill, near the chorten honoring Babu Sherpa, Gary placed the lacy sampler and the rosary atop Shannon's memorial chorten along with a yellow silk *khata*.[12]

Like Babu Chiri Sherpa before them, Team Everest '03 climbed for a purpose greater than the ascent itself.

They too climbed to raise awareness, and in the hopes of better lives. They climbed to celebrate the choices Shannon's family made for her. They climbed for others with unique challenges like theirs to be afforded the same choice.

They climbed in recognition that Shannon's life had meaning and worth and dignity. "Her life represents the true meaning behind Team Everest '03, from my point of view: the freedom for anybody to live in the community of their choice," Gary said.

They climbed to show the world that the true measure of disability is not found in the physicality of a person, but in their spirit.

The vision must be bigger than one person, and its core purpose can never be forgotten or compromised. In its core purpose, it illuminates and lifts all who are a part of it.

THREE

A Team of Leaders

MAKE

Encourage mistakes at the lowest and least vested phase of the journey

OTHERS

Choose others carefully and with purpose

GREATER

Be the one that others hope to carry

Men wanted for hazardous journey. Small wages, bitter cold, long months of complete darkness, constant danger. Safe return doubtful. Honour and recognition in case of success.

> —Ad to attract crew member applications for the
> Trans-Antarctic Expedition of 1914

PARA CIMA

Lukla rests at 9,383 feet.

At elevations above 8,200 feet, the body becomes aware that it's receiving less oxygen. Its response is to increase blood flow to the brain. When it sends too much, a condition called Acute Mountain Sickness (AMS) occurs. AMS is caused by a swelling of the brain, inducing symptoms of headache, exhaustion, shortness of breath, and nausea or vomiting.

Immediate descent is recommended should a climber experience any of these symptoms. If they decide to ignore them and go on, the dangers only heighten.

When a brain that's swollen as a result of AMS reaches the 10,000-foot mark, the threat level increases dramatically. On a scale of one to ten, it becomes a nine.

A condition called High Altitude Cerebral Edema (HACE) can also set in. Its symptoms include profoundly inhibited mental function, hallucinations, loss of coordination, impaired speech, severe headaches, nausea and vomiting, and coma.

There are only two treatment options for this condition: immediate and rapid descent or the use of a hyperbaric oxygen chamber.

When climbers continue on, the danger scale moves from nine to fifteen. The risk of then experiencing High Altitude Pulmonary Edema (HAPE) is very real, and it exists even for climbers who never exhibited signs of AMS or HACE at the lower altitudes.

HAPE can also occur beginning at 8,200 feet.

As the oxygen-deprived body attempts to normalize, it also diverts blood flow to the lungs. The subsequent buildup of fluids creates a potentially deadly situation if the first symptoms (which are flu-like in nature) are missed or ignored.

HAPE symptoms present as extreme shortness of breath, very rapid heart rate, exhaustion, pale complexion, constant coughing, and gurgling sounds coming from the chest.

Death can arrive rapidly once HAPE sets in. Immediate descent is vital.[13]

The above represents the very real risk of death faced by climbers with healthy-function respiratory systems. The risk is (of course) compounded in those with compromised systems.

With any cervical or high thoracic injury, the likelihood of respiratory system impairment is very high. The degree of impairment will depend on the level of spinal injury.

Injuries between T6 and T12 may not affect breathing, but the ability to cough will likely be impaired. Coughing is important, as it's helpful in clearing the airways at altitude.

With injuries between C4 and T6, the intracostal muscles may be either weakened or paralyzed. Breathing therefore may be done solely by the diaphragm. Coughing (especially for persons with quadriplegia) may be difficult or require assistance.

BUTCH CASSIDY & THE SUNDANCE KID

Today is supposed to be a day of rest and altitude acclimation. Some will push the envelope and test their boundaries.

Gary and Lakpa walked together through the town of Lukla, from worlds apart and yet so much the same. In the year that Tenzing Norgay and Sir Edmond Hillary had risen, a part of Lakpa Dorje Sherpa fell. He had been bitten by a cobra, his right arm paralyzed and eventually taken.

Next to Lakpa is Gary, cheerful and inquisitive as ever. In his broken Sherpa-speak, he asks Lakpa about his town, about his family, if he has a wife. Lakpa answers with only nods and smiles.

Though they struggle to communicate, they share a common bond. Lakpa having lost his right arm as a child and Gary having lost his left makes them appear as "one whole person" to the villagers they pass along the way.

Back at camp, the Sherpa rush behind Riley's chair in an effort to help him up a small incline as he struggles, wheels spinning out. He waves them off and eventually reaches his new friend, Matt. There they talk a little about the Sherpa, the pride they take in their responsibilities, how they jump into action at the first sign of struggle.

To be of service is an important part of their duty-bound culture.

Foretelling of what's to come, Matt says to Riley: "There's nothing wrong with a little struggle. That's what it's all about." A smile spreads slowly across his face.

Then he adds: "I'm thinkin' about heading into town. You game?"

Minutes later, Riley sits in his chair overlooking a short stone walkway. It's the first obstacle he encounters on his way to downtown Lukla. Matt eggs him on as he edges out of his seat and onto the ground.

"Show me something."

What happens next proves to be a microcosm of the journey to base camp, a miniature version of the grand pursuit to follow.

If Riley were able to stand, it would've taken only five strides downward to navigate the steps below him. Nothing for him or Matt, or for Gene, Barry, or Mark is that simple. As he carefully places his body on the ground, the Sherpa circle the outer edges of the stairway looking on, wondering what they should do.

From his perch above the highest step, Riley lifts himself up by his hands and scoots his unresponsive lower half to the first step below. Two Sherpa sprint to his aid.

"He's got it, he's got it," says Matt in the background. The Sherpa step away.

In just five short minutes, a dichotomy of purpose unfolds amongst the Sherpa. Riley has now reached the midpoint of the steps with Barry below him and Matt descending from above. Matt holds his body steady with one arm while dangling his wheelchair down the step to a waiting Riley below. Riley will in turn do the same, dropping the chair to a waiting Barry.

The Sherpa watch, at once in conflict with their intense sense of responsibility to the climber's safety, which serves a purpose contrary to the collective will of the chair-passing trio. The Sherpa exchange words with one another. Some are of assurance. Some are of warning.

The chair crashing into Barry. His injury. Their failure to protect the climbers. These things are all foretold in the worried stares of the Sherpa as they watch, their jobs and their honor on the line. To the Sherpas' relief, Matt and Riley reach Barry at the bottom of the stairs, tired but unhurt.

Next, a more complicated and winding set of fifteen stairs. Matt lying on his back leaning upward to catch the chair rolling down at him. Sherpa surrounding them, the expedition's doctor warning them.

Onward they go ...

In another part of camp, two friends are reunited.

Gene Rodgers had once before visited the remote Himalayan kingdom. In 1992, many years after he'd lost all feeling below his neck after a fall, he'd been carried through the lower elevation trails by a group of porters along with their leader.

As the TE '03 airplane arrived in Lukla, he thought he'd recognized some of the men helping him off the plane. He dismissed it to wishful thinking, to his need to feel something familiar in a faraway place.

He experienced the feeling again when they rounded the corner to camp. Then he knew it to be real. It was Tsering Sherpa standing before him, and it'd been Tsering's porters at the airport. His friends from the previous journey were here to greet him.

And to help him.

CARUSO

In 2003 John C. Maxwell wrote *The 17 Indisputable Laws of Teamwork Workbook*.[14] The first in his list of laws is outlined in Chapter One, titled "The Law of Significance: One Is Too Small a Number to Achieve Greatness."

In it, he tells the story of Lilly Tartikoff, once a gifted ballet dancer. Her evolution from the theater stage (as a member of the New York Ballet company) to the world stage as a leading force in the causes of breast and colon cancer research is testament to Maxwell's lesson.

In the course of Lilly's pursuit for a cure, she would join forces with UCLA, Revlon, and eventually Katie Couric. Lilly Tartikoff would help to form the Revlon/UCLA Women's Cancer Research Program, the National Women's Cancer Research Alliance, and the National Colorectal Cancer Research Alliance.

Maxwell states: "The belief that one person can do something great is a myth. Even the Lone Ranger wasn't really a loner. Everywhere he went, he rode with Tonto."

Setting aside some notable exceptions, such as Nelson Mandela and Mahatma Gandhi (for example), Maxwell makes a compelling point.

Sir Ernest Shackleton, like Mandela and Gandhi, is another notable exception to Maxwell's rule; however, Shackleton understood the importance of the many. His methods in choosing a team were at times unconventional, but he possessed an uncanny knack for finding the exact right people. He knew how important it was.

In the months before his expedition set sail, Shackleton tackled the important task of choosing his crew. Nearly 5,000 men had answered his ads. From these he would choose just thirty.[15]

Prevailing wisdom would dictate that he hire a young, able-bodied crew. After all, they would be best suited physically for the demanding terrain and inclement weather they stood to face. Instead he sought out the "old dogs." He believed that when things got scary, the "old salts" were more inclined to keep composure. Their calm in the face of danger would be a good influence on the others.

Maintaining high morale was important to Shackleton.

For his second in command, marks for loyalty, reliability, and shared vision were given highest value. The person he chose was later described by crew members as the second most popular man on the expedition.

He was a man Shackleton knew well – and trusted.

Sir Ernest had led the Nimrod expedition years before, and then had hired well-seasoned, experienced captains who inevitably proved themselves unable. He vowed not to repeat this error; therefore, this time he didn't choose his captain based on experience. Instead he made his choice because the candidate shared his vision and his love of exploration. He chose a man described by others as both bold and eccentric. He was also someone who told a good joke – and liked a good laugh.

In Shackleton's view compatibility mattered as much as experience.

Once key positions were assigned, his second-in-command was instructed to sort the remaining crew applicants' telegrams into three piles – mad, hopeless, and possible. Only those from the "possible" pile were shown to the Boss (as the crew would later lovingly refer to him). The Boss then hand-selected the candidates he liked and conducted personal interviews with each.

He asked the candidates many questions, these among them: *Do you have varicose veins? Are your teeth good? Do you have a good temperament?* and *Can you sing?*

To the final question one candidate replied: "Not like Caruso, but well enough."

The Boss loved happy people; this was a requirement in order to be a part of his expedition. When asked, he was quoted as saying: "Loyalty comes easier to a cheerful person than one with heavy countenance."

Above all other traits, The Boss sought those who demonstrated an intense desire to do the job. He knew that these rare individuals would stay committed even when trouble arose, and that they would do whatever was needed, regardless of how menial the task.

The Boss built his expedition's crew one hand-selected person at a time. The rest, as they say, is history.

The expedition would prove to be more than history. It would become historic.[16]

S C O O B

Gary pulled his van into the parking lot of WalMart, on his way to meet another potential team member. They'd agreed to a lunch interview, after which Gary would decide if Matt Standridge's application to join Team Everest '03 would be accepted.

Matt joined him by the front door and together they exited the building. What happened next abruptly ended the interview.

As Gary describes it, Matt screamed across the parking lot to Gary's 1984 Toyota van (which Gary describes as a Scooby Doo mobile.)

When Gary opened the sliding side door and turned to help Matt, he found that Matt had already latched on and begun pulling the chair and himself inside. He wore a wide infectious grin on his face.

Positive attitude? Check.

Resourcefulness? Check.

Intense desire to be a part of the team? Check.

Gary told Matt, "We don't need to go to lunch. You're in," to which Matt responded by landing back in his chair, promptly popping onto his back wheels and doing a wheelie.

Matt performed another wheelie before being loaded onto the plane en route to Lukla. It would become one of his trademark moves.

Gary selected his good friend Nima Dawa Sherpa as the climbing *sirdar* for the expedition. In anticipation of TE '03's arrival, Nima Dawa had chosen his team of porters and assistants (Gene's friends among them). Nima Dawa, Gary's trusted friend and climbing partner, would be in charge of the day-to-day operations of the Nepalese support team.

Nima and his team greeted the plane as it arrived. Many of the Sherpa that Nima assembled had never seen a wheelchair. Nima patiently instructed them as the plane emptied.

Hours later, after having successfully descended both ancient stone stairways, Matt and Riley sat atop a concrete walkway. Its angle, a sharp forty-five degrees, would prove treacherous for one of them.

BANJO

The field of Positive Psychology has grown exponentially in its value and efficacy over the past ten years. Founder Dr. Martin Seligman centers its focus on helping people become happier, rather than fixing dysfunctional and abnormal behaviors.

Studies performed by Professor Barbara Fredrickson help to illustrate why Positive Psychology principles have been incorporated into the Army's Comprehensive Soldier Fitness approach as an emerging answer to the proactive prevention of PTSD (as well as being incorporated into the reactive treatment of PTSD).

In 2002 Professor Fredrickson conducted a study[17] on the effects of positive and negative emotions on choice. She found that negative emotions created zero-sum thinking – the belief that there's only a winner and loser in every situation. This is to say that zero-sum thinkers never saw the myriad of possibilities in between.

Conversely, positive emotions facilitated creativity, risk taking, and open mindedness. More importantly, they led to non-zero-sum thinking – the belief in win-win outcomes. Simply put, people with positive outlooks saw possibility, rather than the predestination of only gain or loss in situations.

Seeing possibility rather than eventuality can make the difference between life and death in a life-or-death situation.

Her study advanced the "Broaden and Build" theory, one that empirical evidence supports. Broaden and Build describes the "progressive positivity effect" that occurs in a person after they have a positive experience. The experience broadens momentary thought-action repertoires, which in turn lead to the formation of more enduring personal resources, ones found to be both transformational and sustainable.

A number of methods have been clinically shown to induce positive affective experiences that result in positive mood episodes lasting for as many as fifteen minutes. These techniques were used with patients suffering from bipolar disorder (as an extreme example). They resulted in improved perception, cognition, and social interaction almost universally across the study group.

Among the clinical "positive mood-inducing methods" are the following: interacting with a positive person, getting positive feedback, receiving an unexpected gift (such as chocolates, flowers, snacks), listening to music, and reading (or watching) an uplifting story.

As an illustration of this theory, when their ship became stuck in the ice, Shackleton gave orders to abandon all unnecessary cargo. Gold pieces and other items The Boss deemed nonessential to survival were thrown overboard, yet he instructed one crew member to keep his banjo and all to keep their diaries.

Music and stories.

JUST LIKE YOU

"When you first arrive, you feel great, but altitude will fool you. And it will kill you. It's that simple," warns Gary. "Better if they learn that here than further upward."

Matt lay face down on a cot, recovering from the day's exertion and suffering from dehydration, his gaze fixed directly below at the ground.

"Any luck finding that contact lens yet, Matt?" Gene asked. Laughter erupted from all the others.

Their impromptu trip to downtown Lukla had been eventful and full of unanticipated lessons. At the top of a sharply declining walkway of fifteen feet, Riley watched Matt glide straight down to the bottom in a near perfect line. Through his lens, Andy watched as Riley's chair careened to the right uncontrollably, chair crashing into the wall before ejecting its occupant. He dropped his camera and sprinted down the ramp to help (along with many Sherpa), permanently blurring the line between being the storyteller and becoming part of the story.

The mood of the Sherpa surrounding Riley betrayed their sense of frustration with the situation – and with one another for allowing it to happen.

Seeing this, Matt began to push his chair. Slowly, deliberately, he moved himself up the forty-five degree incline one inch at a time in defiance of its steepness.

He said nothing when he reached the top. His glance back down the slope toward Riley and the Sherpa said it all:

We fall, we get back up. Just like you.

Moments later Riley too began to ascend the steep incline, waving off all assistance as he rolled upward toward Matt.

They'd learned a valuable lesson: Heed the knowledgeable warnings of others.

Matt, Riley, and the others listened intently to and followed every one of Gary's pre-trip instructions the next day.

SOMETIMES CREAM,
SOMETIMES SUGAR

Gene waits in the field above, his blue down coat and layers beneath it making him appear plumped, like Violet after she ate the gum in Willy Wonka's Chocolate Factory. He waggles the handless sleeve of his jacket as he jokingly commands the group, "Follow me." He waggles the other sleeve next, then crosses them in what may have been a nod to the Scarecrow in *The Wizard of Oz*.

After the expedition, Gene is interviewed about this moment. He explains that from this point on in the journey, the terrain will be rugged enough to ensure that he'll rarely be in his wheelchair. He'll be carried instead on the back of a Sherpa.

He'll ride in a handmade wicker basket called a *doko*, a device with a remarkably ergonomic and efficient design. For balance, the Sherpa tie a piece of sturdy cloth or cord (trumpline) across their forehead, then backward and around the upper third of the doko. Gene's head, shoulders, and upper torso will rise above those of his Sherpa porter. His legs will align roughly with the Sherpa's shoulders, with knees and toes pointing backward. He'll rarely see where they're going, only where they've been.

Each porter will carry Gene for fifteen, maybe twenty minutes before they trade off. This scene will play across the entirety of their 21-day trek.

At the end, the Sherpa will thank Gene for the honor of carrying him. He was an inspiration, not a burden to them. The Sherpa consider it a great privilege to carry him.

"Sometimes, when I have coffee I have sugar," Gene said. "Sometimes I have cream. I like to live dangerously." As a person with quadriplegia, he had been to forty-nine states and visited seven continents. He'd gone skydiving and scuba diving.

As he rode in the doko, the greatest journey of his life unfolded, one that crossed cultural lines, uniting the thirty-five represented casts of Sherpa in their quest to bring him upward.

Gene, however, would never reach base camp.

FOUR

PERSEVERANCE

MAKE

Look to the analogous for the patterns others can't see

OTHERS

Protect and defend morale at all cost

GREATER

Recognize and appreciate the sacrifice of others in pursuit of common goals

He was young in age, but he was a man. Some mornings he'd show up with his uncle. When his uncle couldn't get out of bed, he'd come alone. In the mountains, cold is no joke. Chaang is Tibetan rice-beer; it's a great remedy for the cold. Sometimes chaang gets used for other reasons. On the mornings after his uncle had too much of it to leave his bed, the yak-boy would step up and take his place. I liked him. I respected that little man. I thought he deserved a reward, so I learned how he liked his hot chocolate. On the mornings he showed up alone I made sure it was just the way he liked it. His job was to carry the grass to feed the yak. If you haven't climbed, this may not seem important. If you don't tend to the yaks at altitude, everything unravels. A climber knows that. The yak carries food, supplies, tents. Without these we don't go on. And a hungry yak is a dangerous yak. They're already a little unpredictable up close sometimes. I took care of the yak-boy because I liked him. I respected him. And because his role was as important as all the others.

—Gary Guller, The Yak-Boy

QUERO DANÇAR

Alexander Fleming returned from vacation on a September day in 1928 to greet an unexpected visitor in his lab. What he found in a discarded pile of plates that rested above the Lysol-line would lead to the discovery of Penicillin, a miracle drug for the 20th century.

Weeks before (and prior to departing on vacation) he'd cleared his workspace so that an associate could use it in his absence. As was protocol, he prepared a tray full of the disinfectant Lysol and carefully placed each of the petri dishes from his desk there, sure to submerge them.

In his absence, his lab assistant made a mess of things. He continued the research that Fleming had tasked him with to be sure, but he never cleaned up after himself. When Fleming returned, an unsightly pile of dirty dishes greeted him.

Fleming was not impressed.

Later that day, the (sloppy) assistant stopped in for a report on his boss' vacation. When Fleming took him to the pile and readied a verbal reprimand, he was stopped in his tracks. The staphylococcus he was culturing was dead. A predator now lived in the petri dishes his assistant had carelessly piled above the Lysol-line.

It was later determined to be the penicillium mold, and the bacterial agent it held had killed the staphylococcus cultures. Penicillin is now estimated to have saved over 82 million lives since its discovery.

Great medical breakthroughs haven't always come from the unexpected. Sometimes the expected hides a greater discovery in plain site, awaiting the one trained eye capable to see it not for what it is, but for where it could lead.

Sixty-seven years after Fleming's discovery, a young neurologist was told in response to his hypothesis: "You're crazy. You're going to get sued. You're going to make people fall. You may even kill someone."

Despite the warnings, he and his team never strayed from their vision.

In the years to come, they too would help many in the course of changing the world's view on stroke rehabilitation. One among them represented the reasons they'd never stopped advancing their program.

Their patient had survived his stroke and soon met the neurologist and his team at the University of Maryland.

When asked what his recovery goals were, the 87-year-old man offered only one. He wanted to dance at his daughter's wedding.

The stroke rehabilitation program, one that others had warned against fourteen years earlier, was now a fully funded Center of Excellence in the treatment and rehabilitation of stroke. When the program met with an unstoppable force (the patient, Mr. M), the result was undeniable.

His daughter would see him dance.

Shannon Ardoin.
Gene.
Mr. M.

To care for, to lift up, and to empower others is to discover the journey's real treasures.

VĪRYA

As Matt's right index finger stretches toward it, the Frisbee arcs away towards Barry. Barry spins it on his left index finger before snatching it down.

It's a rock star catch.

I freeze the frame so I can take in the entire scene. Downward from the Frisbee, below his outstretched arm, Barry's face is locked in a broad smile of accomplishment.

As I watch this part of the documentary, I learn that it's been four years since Barry's vehicle rolled over while he was in the service of his country. Next, I watch Barry playing a full-contact game of rugby in a gymnasium. In the voiceover he explains how hard his wife and children have pushed him to stay active since the accident, how they've helped him get to where he is today. From his days in Alaska to his service in the military, he'd always been adventurous and active.

His wife and daughter are the accelerant added to Barry's already burning fire, the post-accident desire to be adventurous again.

A flash to his daughter, arms raised in a victorious gesture as her dad does something cool-worthy on the rugby field. Like father, like daughter – it's the same triumphant pose Barry strikes with Frisbee in hand.

On the trip to base camp, Barry doesn't want to be pushed, or to be pulled, or to sit on the back of a yak.

After reaching base camp, he would only accept the help that was unavoidable on the day he crested the Khumbu Icefall while blazing a trail for the others to follow.

In Tibet they say: "The peak of a mountain is not too high, and the bottom of the ocean is not too deep, as long as you have exertion. The steepest hill is no higher than a single step."

On April 9, 2003, at the end of their journey, the steepest icefall would prove to be no higher than a single pull.

DRIVING

In 2010, Accenture (a business consulting firm) conducted a study of 674 executives.

Nearly half of all the participants expressed low levels of confidence in their company's ability to quickly adapt to market shifts. Half also indicated little confidence in their company's ability to embrace change in a positive, constructive manner.

And last, 44% weren't certain their company could properly adjust to economic downturn.[18]

These are concerning statistics, considering nearly every business failure is in fact attributable simply to a failure to adapt.

Taken down to its root, corporate adaptability is the cumulative end result of the individual member's collective ability to embrace process evolution and innovation. Both should be done proactively. Often they're forced on an organization, triggering a reactive response.

Regardless of cause, this evolution runs contrary to a basic cognitive function we're all hardwired with: that of First Nature and Second Nature.

Behavioral Scripting defines the myriad small sub-routines we do throughout the day, processes that require us to exert little or no conscious thought.

We pour coffee. We glance at our email. We banter at the water cooler. We complete expense reports. And more.

We begin to form the "scripting habit" early in life, and as we age, the scripts advance from simple to complex. As we gain experience and expertise in our respective professions, we apply scripts to a wider array of more elegant and complex tasks.

At the simplest of levels, behavioral scripting is best understood as a defense mechanism.

Imagine commuting to work every day without it. Every depression or release of the gas and brake pedals, every turn of the wheel would require conscious, directed thought before it could occur.

The end result: a flood of stimulus. A cognitive overtaxation.

An overload.

Take this concept through the workday, to every previously auto-piloted or multitasked process. The corporate wheels would soon stop turning without behavioral scripting.

Scripting allows us to better focus on the "important things." When a learned competence can be performed without thought-effort, the mind is freed to be attentive to the things we interpret as more worthy of our attention.

The problem is, scripting becomes a reflex reaction, one that often elicits a reflexive response. The "But we've always done it this way" retort.

Behavioral scripting is therefore a key driver of change-resistant behavior. It's a very basic, preprogrammed, and (often) fundamentally automated thought process that we develop at a very young age. It's something we often aren't even consciously aware of as it plays out across the day.

The scripts can be rewritten. The rewrite process begins with open, honest, and direct communication.

BECAUSE WE CAN'T

"We all dance to the music that plays in our mind. We can't always choose the tune, but we can surely adjust the notes. If we choose to."

—Gary Guller, March 30, 2013

There were times when it seemed as though the TE '03 expedition could all fall apart.

Such a moment happened days into the journey, when Gary assembled the Sherpa support team for an important conversation.

"There's been some wrestling within our team. These problems need to be addressed. If money's the problem, we can fix that. If you're carrying too much weight, we can fix that too. If it's more than you bargained for, we can agree to terminate. But if we're gonna go through this tomorrow, the day after, at 15,000 feet and 16,000 feet, let's be real clear with one another at this moment that I'm not gonna stand for that for a second. Because we can't."

And the Sherpa knew he was right.

The Tibetans tell the story of *The Prince and the Pauper*. Unlike the Americanized version, the prince and pauper are one – the same person. By a twist of fate, the prince lives his early life as a pauper. As pauper, he greets the day thinking only of himself. *What about me, where will I stay, what will I eat?* This is *lotok* – a "backward" view of life. Thinking only of oneself draws away blessings just as a magnet draws away iron.

Then one day he discovers that he's of royal blood, a member of the royal family, destined to rule the kingdom.

And his world changes.

Natural energy flows through him, and happiness is achieved as the pauper surrenders his "me" view and replaces it with the compassionate *nyingje* – the spirit of a noble heart.

The two were always the same, the prince and pauper. The only real change was in his perspective.[19]

The Tibetans believe that we are all princes and paupers, that we all face a similar choice between *me* and *nyingje*.

PAYU

In Dublin, Ireland, the Senior Conservator of the National Gallery of Ireland enters a Jesuit house and is struck by what he sees. It's 1990, and Sergio Benedetti has arrived to inspect a painting for restorative purposes.

There's no mistaking what's before him. It's a painting of "The Taking of Christ" by Caravaggio.

Surely it must be a copy. After all, the original is a masterpiece, a famously vanished work of European art. Surely it couldn't be here, in plain view of so many, and for so long.

Three years later there's no doubt of its authenticity. A great mystery is solved.

Twenty-two years pass, then after two years of rigorous analysis, a stash of over 1,378 sketches and paintings are found to contain 100 original Caravaggio works. The rest of the artwork belongs to his mentor Simone Peterzano and to Peterzano's other students.[20]

The worth of this collection is an estimated $935 million.

The paintings and sketches had lived in Castello Sforzesco in Milan, Italy, since 1924. Eighty-six years later they caught the attention of Maurizio Bernardelli Curuz Guerrieri, artistic director of the Brescia Museum Foundation. For two years he and his associate painstakingly noted the many similarities (something he terms Caravaggio's "structural DNA") between the Sforzesco collection and known Caravaggio paintings.

"Every artist has a matrix style, unique to them that is distinguishable through the postures and body types in their sketches. They memorize them as students, learning by force of repetition, and carry them into maturity for their later works," said Bernardelli.[21]

It becomes clear; unmistakably clear. The DNA was that of Caravaggio.

How is it possible that "The Taking of Christ" hung over a fireplace in plain view and unrecognized since the 1930s? How did the one hundred sketches at Sforzesco avoid recognition for more than eighty-six years?

In much the same way as people sometimes fail to see others for what they truly are.

They stand as the paintings did, works of art unrecognized, awaiting the trained eye of the person who patiently invests the time to recognize their true potential.

THE TRAIN

As Gary looked across the group of Sherpa he'd just finished addressing, he saw some paupers and some princes. Over the coming days there would remain only princes.

The view of some members of the Sherpa team had been on the "me." It's an understandable perspective, if you put yourself in their place for a moment.

Many had never seen a wheelchair prior to the team's arrival. For days they'd lifted these unfamiliar metal objects up steep inclines and over extremely rocky terrain. Their backs were strained from the unusual angles they'd had to bend themselves in order to lift the team members in their chairs.

The occupied doko were heavy, and at altitude they taxed the endurance of the mountain-capable Sherpa in a way they hadn't experienced before. During times of rest, or when they traded carriers, great care had to be taken in how the doko was placed. Several times the doko's occupant angled too far forward. Sometimes a cliffside and a several-thousand-foot fall lay below, and the doko was righted just in time for its occupant to escape the imminent fall and certain death beneath.

The Sherpa had never worked so hard for a team before, but what Gary said to them that day jarred the handful of pauper Sherpa from their me-state.

They looked again at the occupied doko, and now saw the person – not the burden.

On the morning the group left Namche, Gary ensured that they all leave together, as a team. He knew that the success of the remainder of the expedition rested on him doing so on this particular morning.

Behind Matt were two Sherpa; he rested his right hand on the one in front of him. The Sherpa discussed their strategy and agreed to let Matt push himself until the mountains came back into view. Then they would pick him up.

Four Sherpa surrounded Riley. They imitated the sounds of a train as they advanced. "Choo Choo," they chimed, followed by genuine laughter.

The stone walkways they climbed were far steeper than any they'd faced before that day (on this expedition). But unlike the climbs before, there was real joy visible in the faces of all of the Sherpa. Chuckles turned to belly laughs at the most unusual times. As they strained to raise Matt up a narrow and extremely steep stone stairway, they counted "one, two ... ten." Then they shared a laugh about it. Matt laughed the hardest.

They turned a corner, and next they carried Matt down a walkway lined by doors to the villagers' houses. They dodged laundry that hung to dry (or more likely to freeze itself stiff). One warned the others to watch for stones or Matt's chair might get broken.

All of their efforts lead them to the base of the final staircase they had to climb in order to leave Namche. It was of rock and dirt, uneven and worn. And it was by far the steepest and highest, appearing to contain over fifty individual steps.

Halfway up Matt grinned. "Maybe we'll all be dominos here in a minute," he said as he looked above at the Sherpa team carrying Riley. The dominos never fell. The group made it through the final twists and turns, and then the Sherpa no longer needed to carry. They were rewarded with miles of clear, mostly level paths that the willing TE '03 members traversed of their own volition.

Further up the trail and later, three chairs came to rest. Their drivers' breaths came back to them slowly as they took in the view. Their joy was unmistakable.

Their rest came to an end when Matt announced: "I'm ready. Bring it," and wheeled himself away. A mile or so later, as he crested a hill, Sherpa cheered him on from above. He arrived with a grin, popping a wheelie at the top.

"Let's do it again," he said.

The group forged on. They were now as one, a team bonded by common purpose and by an appreciation for each other.

A L I

In his book *Acres of Diamonds*, Russell Herman Conwell[22] shares a story he was told while traveling down the Tigris and Euphrates rivers.

The guide who led his camel was apparently full of stories. They were both continuous and contiguous according to Conwell. Most of them he allowed to drone off into background noise.

One story, however, had a profound effect on Conwell and eventually on the 1,674 young men and women who were put through college by its retelling.

It's the story of Ali Hafed, a farmer who owned a spacious property full of orchards, gardens, and fields of grain. Hafed was a wealthy man and lived a contented life. That is, until his want for more eventually led to the loss of everything.

During one of his weekly trips to town for supplies, he encountered a stranger. They struck up a conversation that began with superficial small talk. The stranger wasn't from the area but had heard of diamonds being discovered on the outskirts of town. He asked Hafed if he'd heard this too. Hafed hadn't but listened intently as the stranger talked more.

He said he'd come to town to search for diamonds. If the stories he'd heard were true, others were finding rocks large enough to buy an entire county with.

Hafed later bid the stranger goodbye. By the time he'd returned home, the idea of discovering a diamond had completely overtaken his imagination. He could own a mansion and live until his death as a lord over men, his life filled with every imaginable luxury.

Within days he decided to sell his farm and use the money he received to fund his elaborate diamond excavation dreams.

His search took him far and wide; it was wildly unsuccessful. He traveled through Palestine and Europe in search of the elusive treasure. Finally, his journey ended in Barcelona, Spain, when he cast himself into the raging sea, thus ending his (recently) poverty-ridden life.

Some time later, the man who'd purchased Hafed's farm led his camel to the garden brook for a drink. There he spotted a large black stone of curious shape and shine. He took it back with him and placed it on his fireplace mantel as a curiosity.

Nearly a year passed before a friend he'd invited to dinner spotted it and in hasty delight rushed to hold it in his hand.

It was a diamond, a most illustrious one at that. The visitor had his friend bring him to the garden and show him the area where the treasure had been found. Together they began shifting the sands below their feet, and as they did they were amazed to see a seemingly endless number of the black shiny rocks in the garden that day.

Hafed's property was named "the diamond mine of Golconda." It would be incredibly productive.

Had Hafed taken the time to first learn what a diamond in its rough form looked like, then taken the time to look at what was literally in front of his eyes every day, he would have retired with all his dreams fulfilled.

OIL

Azim Premji would become the person who'd make the largest cumulative philanthropic donation in history. On the day he signed the Giving Pledge, a 12% stake in the company was shifted and $2.3 billion dollars moved to his education-centered trust. It would more than double his previous donation efforts.

He had taken over leadership of the Wipro Company at the age of twenty-one on the death of his father. He'd just graduated Stanford with a degree in Electrical Engineering. Shortly after taking the leadership reins, he put his audacious plans for the company into action.

Wipro was formed in 1947 as a vegetable oil company. Premji reimagined it as a consumer goods company. By 1975 its annual sales exceeded $2 million, and it had grown beyond consumer brands to the manufacture of hydraulic and pneumatic cylinders.

In 1977 Wipro expanded into information technology. It next followed the natural progression from IT to computers, then to software.

Wipro is today the largest outsourced R&D Services provider and remains in the forefront of advancement in remote IT services.

Azim Premji began his trust in 2001 with an initial donation of $125 million in company shares. In early 2000 he added an additional $2 billion.

The trust funded a number of social not-for-profit initiatives, including improved equality and stronger primary education systems. To date, Premji's charitable donations have reached $4.4 billion. Premji remains an outspoken advocate in the cause of social good.[23] It's said that he lives a modest life, having just traded in his Toyota for a used Mercedes.

His friend Kiran Mazumdar-Shaw, Managing Director and Chair of Biocon Limited, told *Forbes* magazine: "Azim has set a trend for others to emulate." Each year Kiran donates half the dividends she receives. She plans to up the ante to 75% according to *Forbes*.

Our Acres of Diamonds are the people who surround us. Just as it was at Ali's farm, they exist all around us, sometimes just beneath a layer of sand that obscures them from our view.

Like Premji, we should invest in them.

T E A

It's the simple things that bring the climbers happiness. The comfort of routine; knowing that each day may bring the unknown, but that each evening the camp will be built again. In the evenings there will be stories, and sometimes dancing and song. And each morning the water will boil and that wonderful piping hot bed tea will soon arrive at their tent.

While all of the above is true, it's not the whole picture. And to leave this chapter on that note simply romanticizes the whole thing in a way that doesn't do it the honor it deserves.

Bed tea doesn't make them push themselves, when being carried is always an option for them. Nor does it magically heal the blisters formed on Matt's, Riley's, Barry's, and Mark's hands from pushing the wheels of a chair mile upon mile.

It doesn't move Dinesh forward a step at a time and alone, last to arrive to camp each and every evening because of the caution he must take in every prosthetic step. It doesn't offer him any relief from the soreness that the jarring of going downhill causes him. Only duct tape provides temporary relief, so he wraps his leg in it each day and goes on.

It doesn't hold Gene in the moments that his body rebels against the altitude. His spinal injuries make it difficult for his body to regulate temperature, so desperate cold is a constant evening visitor.

It certainly isn't the thing that brings Gary back just two years after his first attempt to summit.

The thing that drives them all is something else.

Gary Guller taking a breather at Camp 1 on Mt. Everest

Team Everest 2003: Mt. Everest Base Camp

Mt. Everest from Summit of Kala Pattar

Sherpa Nap with Team Everest members

Team Everest Member Barry Muth looking strong

Team Everest Member Matt Standridge
with his infectious smile

Team Everest Member Matt Standridge being awesome

Tibetan Prayer Flags

Nima Dawa Sherpa checking in with base camp

Lakpa Dorje Sherpa in Namche Bazaar

Mt. Everest from Summit of Mt. Cho Oyu

Namgyl Sherpa

Nima Dawa Sherpa departing Camp 3 on Mt. Everest

Gary Guller on the way to Camp 1 on Mt. Everest

Team Everest 2003 Signature Banner on Summit of Mt. Everest

Lungta

Gary Guller at the finish line of the 25th Marathon des Sables

Gary Guller and Lama Geshe

Gary Guller and Nima Dawa Sherpa after Mt. Everest Summit
Tired at Camp 4

Gary Guller and Pem Tenji Sherpa with Texas flag
on Summit of Mt. Everest

Da Ningyma Sherpa high on Mt. Everest near South Summit

Gary Guller notifying base camp that the team is standing on the Summit of Mt. Everest

Gary Guller tired after Summit push

Summit of Mt. Everest

Mt. Makalu (World's 5th Highest Mountain)
from high on Mt. Everest

Camp 1 Mt. Cho Oyu (World's 6th Highest Mountain)

Gary Guller climbing over Amphu Laptsa Pass

Gary Guller on Summit of Cho Oyu
(World's 6th Highest Mountain) with Brook Alongi

Pem Tenji crossing icefall ladder

Nima Dawa Sherpa sporting his new glasses

Porba Sherpa offering warm drinks

Gary Guller serving up peanut butter and jelly bagels

Nima Dawa hungry after
Mt. Everest Summit

Nima Dawa Sherpa after
too much Tabasco!

Gary Guller on the
Summit of Mt. Everest
with card of Mt. Kailash
from Lama Geshe

Departing Camp 1
Mt. Cho Oyu
(World's 6th Highest
Mountain)

Gary Guller speaking to disability non-profit in Kathmandu

Mt. Everest at Sunrise

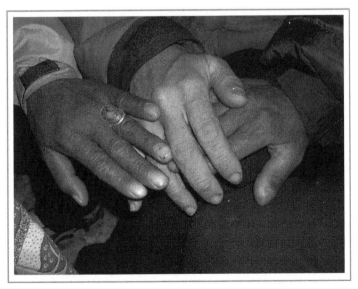

Sherpa Brothers

FIVE

Lungta

MAKE

Inspire others to give back

OTHERS

Encourage the small conversations

GREATER

Be in the service of others

I t takes 1/100th of a second to change an person's entire day. You pour your coffee, walk up to the counter and slam your change down to pay, then walk away and onto the day's business … or you take that 1/100th of a second to smile at the person working behind the counter, the one who probably got up at 3 a.m. that day to go to work to pour the water and measure the grounds for the cup you just bought to be fresh and ready for you. And maybe, in that 1/100th of a second, your smile makes a difference to that person. Maybe it makes them a little happier in that moment. Maybe they go on to give that smile back to the next people in line. Maybe that's how one person can effect change in the world, 1/100th of a second at a time.

—Gary Guller, The Coffee Story, February 5, 2013

STROLLERS

In 2012, after the two-year study they'd commissioned under the MNW (Measuring National Well-Being) program was complete, the British government began monitoring a new national statistic next to its GDP.[24]

The official governmental recognition of the importance of its people's General Well-Being is now a reality. Shortly after learning of the British study, Canada and France began investigating their own General Well-Being programs.

Why has it taken until now to hit the national consciousness, when emotional contagion (EC) is such a familiar occurrence?

We've all experienced it. We make a goofy face at an infant in the stroller next to us, and they scrunch their face trying to figure out just what we did. As they grow older they mimic the face. And so it begins, carrying through to adulthood. We laugh; others around us soon join in. We cry; others' eyes well up. We're angry, and the room around us darkens.

One study was commissioned to specifically place a dollar value on another simple and common emotive.

A smile.

Prior to being asked to make a purchasing decision, one of two pictures was flashed before the study's participant at speeds too fast for them to consciously register. One picture showed a frowning face; the other, a broad smile. They next sampled an unlabeled beverage and were asked what retail price they'd be willing to pay for it.

The individuals shown the "smiling person" picture were willing to pay more.

The theory that happier, healthier people create a more robust economy is proving to be true. There also appears to be a direct economic correlation between Life Satisfaction and Real Household Actual Income.[25]

1/100th of a second.

That's all it takes.

And it's free.

APRIL 9TH

The Sherpa rose early. They had important things to do.

Their 21-day trek was over and their work was complete. Yet they'd decided to do one last thing before they all descended, one that required the Sherpa to continue in service rather than to rest.

Just two days earlier, the team arrived at base camp. It was the day of my 41st birthday and a full ten years before I'd complete this book. They'd beaten the odds. Villagers once speculated that the team wouldn't make it more than two or three days. Even some team members had their doubts.

On her arrival, member Christine White said: "Everyone had their struggles. But we're here, and we really do have one voice with which we can tell the disabled community and the world: It can be done."

Over 15% of the world's population is given the label of "disabled." Yes, it was an empowering message to this group.

It can be done.

The message goes far further, to far more, taking into account that more than 35.7% of all Americans are obese[26] (CDC) and 45.3 Americans don't exercise regularly.[27] Clearly the message needs to get out, considering many "able-bodied" people don't walk further than their refrigerators and couches after work, and some even drive their car down the driveway to their mailbox to get the day's mail.

Real disability is measured in the limits we place on ourselves, regardless of our physical condition. The truly disabled are those who don't try to use their bodies and minds to the potential they each have, whatever that may be.

◆   ◆   ◆

Toward the end of their trek through the rock and scree slopes of the Khumbu Glacier, they got their first glimpse of the gateway to the Everest summit.

The deadly Khumbu icefall.

The team listened with a measure of awe as avalanches roared in the slopes above them. They looked around at a view no picture could capture, certainly none they'd seen before departing Austin.

Every member of the team who arrived that day had done so in pursuit of something very personal, something that was different for each of them.

Their own individual Everest base camp conquest.

Barry Muth would say that while experiencing Everest, he would learn about himself and his injury. He would come to know what he could do and how hard he could push himself. He would test the limits and know the boundaries.

The greatest satisfaction they each would find was in being a part of their team's accomplishment, of being a part of this unique group, of cheering each other on, pushing each other forward, giving each other assurance. The friendships formed and the common bond struck would be the prize pennant that each wore home.

And this was all not lost on the Sherpa. They'd watched this group over these 21 days, with a growing respect for the team's commitment to the journey – and to each other.

The Sherpa would reward them with a gift, something else that a group like theirs had never done. They would give the team ice-climbing lessons at the Khumbu icefall.

Nima Dawa had approached Gary the evening before to discuss the idea. It was clear that the Sherpa understood the vision of the Team Everest expedition, and they'd collectively decided to stretch that vision even further beyond base camp.

JOINING THE RIGDEN
KING AND QUEEN

The Sherpa (a western mispronunciation of the ethnic designation Shar-wa) migrated from Tibet to the Solu-Khumbu region in the 16th century, in large part to escape the warfare that was occurring.

Their name literally means "people of the East." Most of them use "Sherpa" as their surname outside of their community as it is internationally recognized – and respected.

The Sherpa's remarkable ability to perform strenuous tasks at altitude is a source of scientific amazement. Though the exact physiological reasons for their unique adaptation to altitude is not known, some studies have shown that they may have a higher hemoglobin level, allowing their bloodstreams to carry and absorb oxygen more efficiently. This facilitates better metabolic function at altitude.

This increased efficiency is evident in their ability to function at very low oxygen-density levels. Some Sherpa summit Everest without the use of supplemental oxygen; some stay at altitude for incredibly long periods without it. Babu Chiri Sherpa, for example, stayed at the peak for a record twenty-one hours without supplemental oxygen.

The Sherpa's unique physical abilities place them in high demand for Everest expeditions. While this offers them a livelihood, the Sherpa have a much deeper and more spiritual connection with Everest.

Money isn't the sole driving force for going up.

To attain enlightenment, the Sherpa believe that they must live in service of others. They climb Everest not for themselves, but in service to the other climbers – to ensure their safety upward and their safe return.

The first of their people to summit Everest was Tenzing Norgay (Sherpa). He described the mountain as warm, friendly, and loving, a depiction others would most likely use to describe a good friend. It's certainly not a portrayal that's used by many (but the Sherpa) to explain a place requiring such physical exertion to reach, one that holds such danger in each of the many steps upward it requires.

The Sherpa don't view Summiting Everest as reaching a goal; it's instead a way for them to draw themselves closer to the Buddhas.

To follow in the path of the Rigden King and Queen is to realize your royal birth, to become a prince. In the legend of Shambhala, the Rigdens are its inhabitants, ones who have never strayed from basic goodness and service to each other. Their king is at once wise and compassionate, even as his countenance conveys a wrathful warrior. On the Rigden King's helmet are four pennants, symbolizing long life, good health, success, and happiness – for others.

Such is the Sherpa way.

PADDLES

When the question of what makes teams function more effectively was raised to them, MIT's Human Dynamics Laboratory[28] began to listen. They listened with technology at a grand scale, across many different types of groups.

Their charge was to determine why groups with similar responsibilities (for example call centers servicing the same company or type of business) could vary so greatly in their effectiveness and in the results they produced. They decided to monitor the groups individually, and to monitor the individual group's members, in an effort to better understand the dynamics at play.

They began by equipping members of each team they studied with (unobtrusive) electronic badges capable of collecting up to one hundred data points per minute on the following: tone of voice, body language, energy levels, and even who they conversed with. They measured many other things as well.

Their findings clearly demonstrated that the higher functioning teams (as measured by revenue performance, KPI[29] metrics, etc.) had distinct success predictors in the ways they communicated with one another.

They found, for example, that the number of person-to-person exchanges between team members caused as much as a 35% variation in the team's performance. The more the better, with several dozen individual conversations per hour among team members being the ideal (more than that caused productivity to be adversely affected).

Though the conversations were brief, they were all apparently quite important.

In the year 2000, the Gallup organization began a study of 1,000 employed adults over the age of 18. For two years they contacted the participants quarterly and have kept contact on a semi-annual basis ever since.

They found that only 29% of the participants could be classified as "actively engaged," while 56% were termed "not engaged," and 15% were "actively disengaged." The contrasts in thinking and behaviors among the three groups was stark.

For example, 59% of the engaged group felt that their job brought out their most creative ideas, while only 3% of the actively disengaged shared that belief. Next, 61% of the engaged group felt that they had a high level of collaborative interaction with their coworkers; not surprisingly, only 9% of the actively disengaged concurred.

When they sought to find the key differentiators between the groups, one statistic clearly delivered the answer. A solid 76% of the engaged group shared workplace friendships, ones built on trust, interaction, and shared thinking. Conversely, only 21% of the actively disengaged group agreed.

There is a hard cost of disengagement in addition to the soft (opportunity) cost of possible future innovations. According to GMJ,[30] nearly 15% of the US workforce was disengaged at the time of their study. This base of approximately 20.6 million workers cost the US economy nearly $328 billion in 2006, the year the study was commissioned.

Finding creative ways to build engagement and interaction isn't just about team building or best HR practice. It's about dollars and cents too.

As leaders and team members, we all intuitively understand the importance of regular and open communication. We may assume that this communication should come in the form of group interaction, and therefore hold regular meetings to facilitate it together with the group and its leader. To the contrary, the MIT study found that the context and quality of individual conversations (outside of the group meetings) were in fact a greater indicator of high-function teams.

Team-level communication is critical, make no mistake; but connections at a personal level make all the difference according to MIT. Encouraging this means making doors stay open – even once in a while interrupting the productive-looking worker sitting solo in their office for an impromptu conversation.

Companies today understand the importance of communication and its role in high-function team performance. It's commonplace to expect every company (not doing business under a rock) to consciously make efforts to improve teamwork, often through team building.

Some, however, invest their time in frivolous and ridiculous team-building activities, such as paddling each other using their rival's yard signs. Meant to motivate sales, the winners of this competition within a California-based alarm company went on to feed the losers baby food, make them wear diapers, and even hit them in the face with pies.

Brilliant.

It almost defies reality to read such a story, knowing that it actually happened, that it wasn't simply a script point in the (nonexistent) *Horrible Bosses 2 – The Alarm Wars*.

Other companies do it right, and they lead the field in high-performance team development. They do so by understanding the things that actually enhance team performance (as opposed to those who paddle – and punish it).

The first, and most basic tenet – *cooperation* among team members (in the early days of the team's formation) – builds teams, whereas *competition* undermines them (unless it's "healthy" competition and the dialog drives "constructive discontent"). In the critical early days of team formation, before deep-rooted (and real) trust is built, building a cooperative dynamic is of paramount importance.

Through cooperation comes acceptance, and the idea that others' ideas are worthy of hearing. This opens the door to frank and honest dialogue and gives confidence to the team that they can express opinions openly, even when they expect dissenting views to arise.

In the acceptance phase, a critical dynamic develops, that of team members developing an appreciation for each other. In doing so, the developing group sees past the individual. The common good comes more clearly into view. As the team forms intimate connections, their interactions allow learning to occur both *from* each other and *with* each other.

In this model, one built in the service of the common good, truly incredible advancements are made.

THE DRAGON'S BACK

CNN calls it the world's hardest foot race. It spans across 250 km (155.343 miles); it occurs across six days, in temperatures often reaching a blistering mid-day 120° F. MdS (Marathon des Sables) is the real deal. Not for the faint of heart. Not for the uncommitted.

You must be self-sufficient to participate. You're given a place to sleep at night; all else is up to you. You carry everything on your back – all of your necessary food and equipment.

Gary runs the race for more than just the challenge.

He runs the race because it offers equanimity. "The race is run with absolutely no discrimination, be it based on nationality, financial resources, sexual orientation, or disability," he says.

He runs the race in honor of his many TE '03 friends, and in the vision they shared of raising awareness.

He runs for the Christopher and Dana Reeve Foundation, which is dedicated to curing spinal cord injury and improving the lives of people living with paralysis.

The extreme heat on the track brings back memories for Gary – some happy, some darker. "Sometimes you jump on the dragon's back, look it in the eyes, and decide who's going to win," he says.

It also brings the understanding of the importance of something small, but momentous. As the runners encounter each other on the trail each day, fighting the common enemies of heat and exhaustion together, they exchange encouraging smiles. They happen quickly, but they feel as though they condense an entire life's determination into the fleeting second of their exchange. They say, without words, "I'm just like you – and we can both make it."

A smile.

THE PACKET

On March 31st the group met a new and inspiring friend. As the 71-year-old Lama Geshe spoke, many realized that they were experiencing the most emotionally significant moment of their journey. They were participating in a ceremony that most every climber since Hillary and Norgay had done before them. Yet this one was theirs. Its message unique to them.

The Sherpa believe that every climber must pay respects to the mountain, the "mother goddess of the world," before their ascent of Everest begins.

The *Puja* is therefore a ceremony of great significance to the Sherpa – and to those hopeful for a safe journey to the summit. It's held at the Tengboche Monastery. One by one, each of the members carries their ceremonial scarves (known as *khatas*) to Lama Geshe for blessing.

Later, in a private ceremony, the lama writes a message on a card in Tibetan. The climbers are to hold up this card to the mountain in order to seek its permission on the day of summit.

The morning after the ceremony, Lama Geshe appeared in the courtyard where the entire TE '03 group was gathered. He encouraged them, saying: "You feel like you are unable to act like others. Feel strong, like I can do everything that others can do. We're all the same, all beings. All one."

Monday, April 7th, on TE '03's arrival at base camp, Lama Geshe met with the smaller group that prepared to ascend Everest. He gave them blessings; he offered advice. Before their time together was over, he gave them something else.

A packet filled with special powders and sacred rice.

THE 9TH, PART TWO

Barry reached the top of the 30-foot hill, surrounded by the Sherpa who'd accompanied him. It had been a brutally demanding climb. He'd reached the top with every ounce of strength he could offer. He'd moved every inch he could under his own power.

The Sherpa had worked hard to make this day possible, to make it possible for Barry to climb. They walked beside him throughout the ascent, watching out for problems, ensuring success. Accompanying him, encouraging him.

They reached the top together, the Sherpa and Barry.

Throughout the morning others would follow, some choosing the 45-degree slope. Matt and Riley – Butch Cassidy and the Sundance Kid – would of course choose the near-vertical ice face to climb.

Atop the 30-foot hill the Sherpa hung a customized American flag, one with stars arranged in the shape of a wheelchair.

The vision of the one had clearly become that of the many.

SIX

IMPERMANENCE

MAKE

The conversation with those you serve trumps the importance of all others

OTHERS

Listen actively. Learn adaptively. Evolve or die.

GREATER

Stick to the proven. Aggressively beta the unproven.

W e had a very merry evening, though it is difficult to find songs that we have not heard many times before.

—Dr. Alexander Macklin, Endurance expedition member

A BOWL OF RICE

Nerve cells fired furiously as adrenaline, noradrenaline, and cortisol coursed through the bloodstream. Blood, urgently redirected, flooded muscles and limbs. Pupils dilated and sight sharpened. All sense of pain and fatigue diminished as impulses heightened.

Death could be imminent.

Moments before, Gary heard a rumbling as he reached the halfway point of the Khumbu Icefall. The mountain often spoke, but rarely with this level of assertiveness. It roared with a voice foretelling of an imminent threat as ice and rock violently ejected from the southwest face of Everest. An avalanche had begun.

Gary and Nima Dawa Sherpa stood directly in its path.

The adrenaline flooding their bodies gave them the illusion that the threat was unfolding in slow motion. In fact, the danger advanced at high speed toward them. They would take action or they would die, buried under a sea of snow, ice, and rock.

Eyes met.

One pair conveyed the insane urgency of the moment. The other offered calm reassurance as Nima Dawa stepped out into the path of the avalanche. Simultaneous to his advancing steps he reached into his jacket pocket, removing precious content. In one motion Nima flung a handful of rice toward the coming flood of ice, rock, and snow.

The rice that Lama Geshe had given him days before.

When Gary saw Nima step into danger he reflexively grabbed the back of his jacket, pulling him under a nearby boulder. There they braced for what was to come.

Together they watched in astonishment as the avalanche redirected itself. Magically it altered its course, and now it passed ten feet to their left. When the danger was gone, the two snow-dusted survivors locked eyes again.

Soon laughter erupted as Gary said: "I'll never look at a bowl of rice the same way again."

Before them lay a trail now altered by the furious rush of dislodged mountain that raged by them moments before.

They would take time to study the new landscape, and once they understood it, they would continue on.

ANICCA

Life is like a river. Every experienced moment adds itself to the next, at once giving the impression of continuous, unified, directional movement, just as flowing water.

This is an illusion.

The river, as life, is in a continuous state of change. The river that existed yesterday is not the same one that exists today. The ground underneath has shifted. The shoreline has changed shape.

The particulates it carries today are gone, replaced anew tomorrow.

Reality is the existing moment. What follows is undetermined and new.

OUVIR

Today, only six of the top 25 companies on the Fortune 500 list from 1961 remain. The average life expectancy of a Fortune 500 company was 75 years just one-half century ago. It's now estimated to be only 15 years. The explosive emergence of new technologies and efficiencies, along with a shift in the balance of power from company to consumer, has created an adapt-or-die environment for businesses.

It's an avalanche of informed consumerism and technological advancements. Companies today must stand defiantly in its path or surrender to its inevitable crushing force. There's no other sustainable option.

Like Nima and Gary, some successfully hold their ground.

Having just been hired and appointed CEO, Lou Gerstner's first months on the job presented crisis. Record losses had occurred the year before due to technological advances that threatened the company's core competency.

Something had to be done.

Quickly.

His predecessor watched as the emergence of personal computing and client-server technologies ate away at the once thriving computer mainframe business that was IBM's mainstay. The new threat to their core competency came not from another Goliath-sized company, but instead from many smaller "Davids."

Nimble, aggressive, and less diversified Davids to be sure.

The former CEO determined that the only possible course of action against the threat of these emerging players was to take apart IBM, to break it into smaller autonomous units, each focused on a single component, such as storage, software, printers, etc. To Akers, this alone would ensure that the company could keep pace with the rapid advancements created by the innovative new breed of competition.[31]

Under his direction, IBM would be split into many Davids, rather than remaining the Goliath it currently was in his eyes.

The Board at IBM had a different vision. They replaced Mr. Akers with Lou Gerstner. It was an interesting choice as Mr. Gerstner's background wasn't in technology, having spent four years as CEO of RJR Nabisco and eleven years as a top executive at American Express. Gerstner would become the first "outsider" hired into upper management since 1914.

Mr. Gerstner wasn't a seasoned expert in computers; his strength was in understanding service. He took inventory of the company's competencies as his first order of business, and quickly surmised that IBM's greatest strength wasn't in its products. To Gerstner, it was in IBM's ability to leverage data in the conveyance of integrated solutions to its clients.

He next needed to understand how he could deliver on this strength in a way that would resonate with the end user.

It was 1993, many years before MIT would perfect the science of listening through technology, before they would prove the importance of the individual conversation over that of the many.

Lacking these advances, and the empirical data they presented, Gerstner trusted his instincts, ones honed from fifteen years in service-focused businesses – instincts that told him the answers to the problems IBM faced resided outside the conversations taking place in the company's offices and meeting rooms.

Outside the doors of corporate headquarters.

Into the offices of their clients.

Despite the intense, urgent pressure on him to stop the financial bleeding, Gerstner purposed himself to first understand the emergence of personal computing from his client's point of view.

What he learned would help chart a new course for the company. It would seed IBM's successful recreation and lead them down a bold new path.

Like Shackleton before him, Gary knew the value of listening. They both viewed their team members as valued contributors to be heard and understood. They, like Gerstner, led according to the needs of others.

FIVE C'S

Anand Mahindra took a big risk in 2003. His family's tractor business had both grown and diversified, but there was an emerging demographic that wasn't met by the Mahindra and Mahindra company's current product portfolio.

The company began in 1945 as a Jeep assembly franchise. It expanded to eventually become one of the world's top three tractor manufacturers.

Mahindra, a Harvard graduate, knew that India was experiencing a boom in its middle class. At the time, KSA Technopak estimated that this emerging demographic commanded $10.5 billion in cash. Cash to burn.[32] Mahindra knew that this "burn" would create a demand in the automotive industry for vehicles that catered to the young, upwardly mobile consumer demographic that was growing exponentially within his country.

In 2003 Mahindra and Mahindra launched the Scorpio. It would become India's first sports-utility vehicle and would soon expand its consumer base around the world. Sales for the Scorpio have grown at a brisk pace, annually at 102% to be exact.

Over the years Anand Mahindra has diversified the company across six distinct market sectors: automotive, farm equipment, infrastructure, financial services, information technology, and engineering design.

Today Mahindra and Mahindra, still a family-owned company, boasts $15.9 billion in annual sales.

On March 11, 2013, the company announced its launch of the "Ask" movement. Ask's purpose is to inspire thought and questions, and to challenge conventional thinking across the intelligent and inquisitive consumer base in India in an effort to drive their vision of the Future of Mobility.

Their goal is to create an efficient automotive ecosystem that is Clean, Convenient, Connected, Clever, and Cost Efficient.[33]

Leaders listen.

FORTITUDINE VINCIMUS

To hear the story for the first time inspires a reflexive reaction.

One of summary disbelief.

The year is 1915. The day is January 18th. Sir Ernest Shackleton and his crew have sailed within a day of their destination.

Their journey began on August 1, 1914, the day Germany declared war on Russia. They depart London, first bound for Buenos Aires, Argentina. They reach it safely, and then depart on August 26th for their next destination – the Grytviken whaling station on the island of South Georgia. They depart Grytviken on December 5, 1914.

Unbeknownst to the crew of the Endurance, this will be the last time they'll set foot on solid ground for the next 497 days.

On January 18, 1915, it all begins. The story of discovery and adventure quickly turns into one of brutal survival.

Against all odds.

As their ship becomes hopelessly wedged in the shifting icepack of the Weddell Sea, all aboard the vessel Endurance come to terms with the knowledge that the masses of frozen water that have gripped their ship have no plans to release their hold. The Endurance is wedged in a way that one crew member later described as being "stuck like an almond in a chocolate bar."[34]

Eight days earlier came their first view of the expedition's destination – Antarctica.[35] Today they would begin the process of watching it disappear. Their ship would be dragged northward and away from Antarctica for the next ten months.

On October 27th, at 5 pm, Shackleton gives the order to abandon ship. The crew watches helplessly as their vessel is pulled to the depths of the ocean.

All that remain are supplies and three small lifeboats.

One crew member keeps his banjo, all others keep their diaries.

For the next four months the crew lives in near total darkness. Their only light is from the moon; it shines brightly through their flimsy tents. The nights are still, save the sound of water freezing.

They exist on diets of penguin, seal, and dog.

Once winter ends, and spring reaches its last days, the warmer sun of summer shines down on the expedition. It melts the ice under their tents. Their body heat melts the snow beneath them when they sleep.

The ice floor is no longer stable enough to support them. It shatters and splinters.

They again take to the water, this time in the three small lifeboats they'd saved from their sinking ship months before.

For the next four months, they'll live on these lifeboats. They'll fight the wilds of the raging water and the monotony of the flat seas.

On April 16, 1916, they finally reach land. It's a stinking guano-covered mass called Elephant Island. Most of the crew survives the storms that relentlessly pound the island by huddling together under two lifeboats, their only refuge from the furious wind and rain.

Shackleton takes the third lifeboat and departs along with five crew members. They set sail to find help.

They travel 800 miles together, across raging waters to the small island they'd visited as the journey began, in a tiny lifeboat not built for such hazards.

On May 16, 1916, they once again reach South Georgia Island. There they'll disembark, and traverse the rugged terrain of the island. They'll climb mountains that are thousands of feet high at their peaks. They'll hike continuously for 36 hours until they again reach civilization. They find it at the Stromness whaling station.

For the first time since their departure 497 days earlier, the world learns of the true whereabouts of the Endurance crew. It has not conquered Antarctica.

Rescue teams are organized.

On May 23, 1916, Shackleton and two others depart on the British-owned Southern Sky in an attempt to reach the stranded crew on Elephant Island. They're stopped in their tracks by heavy ice just 100 miles from shore.

On June 10th the Uruguayan government lends the Instuto de Pesca No. 1 to the rescue efforts. The ice pack thwarts their mission as well.

Next, the schooner Emma sets sail for Elephant Island. It departs on July 10th, but it too falls 100 miles short, the victim of icepack and storms.

In what would prove to be the final rescue mission, the Chilean government lends the steamer Yelcho to the effort. It sets sail with Shackleton aboard on August 25th.

On August 30, 1916, the Yelcho successfully reaches Elephant Island to find the entire crew alive.

All alive.

When interviewed later about the harrowing two years they survived in the brutal, freezing Arctic, the crew describes it in a most unexpected way. They tell of the fun they had. They tell tales of their camaraderie, of the best jokes they heard. Some describe their time as the most memorable and enjoyable days of their lives.

Crew members (while still aboard the Endurance) elaborately decorated their cabins. They had contests for creativity and gave rewards to the winners.

Birthdays and Christmases were festively celebrated. Competitive games of ice hockey were played. The men even waxed poetic, often reading their prose to each other during meals and at night.

The crewmen's diaries didn't contain words of doom and gloom – not when they were stranded on the ice for ten months, not when their ship sank, and not when they lived aboard the lifeboats. Instead, they wrote about the little things that happened throughout their days. They talked of the books they'd read, even described in detail what the weather was like.

Dr. Macklin wrote about the enjoyment the crew shared during the weekly concerts Shackleton arranged.

The banjo was precious cargo indeed.

Often they wrote of Shackleton, in praise of all he was to them.

When asked how they were able to survive for two years in the harshest and most unforgiving of climates, and under the most impossible of scenarios, they said: "Shackleton."

Everything Shackleton did, beginning with the methods he used in the selection of his crew to the way he communicated and interacted with them, the way he assigned tasks through the equipment and supplies he chose to bring, everything led to the inevitable ending.

His crew's safe return.

INNOVATIONS

By contrast, the crew members of the Franklin expedition of 1845 never had the opportunity to talk about their leader. They'd instead write about the demise of their expedition in notes that would be discovered fifteen years after their deaths.[36]

In May 1845, Franklin and crew set sail aboard two vessels: the HMS Erebus and the HMS Terror. The crew numbered 129. The provisions could last a hefty seven years. The expedition carried new innovations, such as a seawater distilling system. All indicators were of success for the well-stocked, high-tech (for their time) adventurers.

Eighteen months later they all mysteriously disappeared. Numerous rescue parties were sent. None found any evidence of them.

Then, in 1859, an expedition dispatched to King William Island happened upon a discovery. They found skeletons that proved to be those of the Franklin crew.

Next to them lay their diaries.

In piecing together the many messages left by the men before their death, it was learned that both ships became stuck in giant ice floes in September of 1846. The men had remained aboard the ship, and slowly they'd begun to die, one by one. Of the handful that remained alive, all but one decided to abandon ship and seek rescue on foot.

The bodies of the men who abandoned ship would be discovered 144 years later, and they would yield evidence of lead poisoning (from the innovative new seawater distilling system they brought with them), starvation, hypothermia, and tuberculosis. They would also leave questions of possible cannibalism.

In January 1911, the Terra Nova expedition set out to reach Antarctica. It's said that every single decision that expedition leader Captain Robert Scott made led to the death of every member of the expedition.[37]

Like Franklin before him, Scott brought innovative new technology with him. In Scott's case it was both experimental and untested. Three motorized sledges accompanied Scott as he set out for the South Pole. They'd been built specifically for Terra Nova, designed to carry all of the expedition's food and equipment.

Days into the journey, the largest (and heaviest) broke through the ice. It came to rest sixty fathoms below, precious cargo with it. Over time the remaining two would malfunction due to the abusive weather's relentless attack on them. Unfortunately for Terra Nova, Scott had decided at the last minute not to bring the sledge's inventor along with them. Subsequently, the machines could not be fixed.

The animals Scott chose to bring therefore burdened the food and equipment that the machines were meant to carry. Unfortunately for Terra Nova, Scott bucked conventional wisdom and chose to use (mostly) ponies instead of dogs to haul the sleds. The ponies proved a poor choice. Sadly, they all died early in the expedition.

This left only the men and a handful of dogs to carry all of the vital necessities. The loads they carried were absurdly heavy, leading to a high incident of physical exhaustion in the men. The food that accompanied Terra Nova was insufficient calorically to properly fuel the overtaxed team members. The process of starvation began, and with it the requisite deterioration of bodies and morale.

Scott attempted to mitigate the issue by leaving some provisions at waypoints along the journey. This (he thought) would ensure them having ample food for the return trip.

The expedition, however, had left without packing snow goggles. Snow blindness and poor navigational instruments caused them to incorrectly mark their waypoints, rendering them undiscoverable on the return trip.

As if all this weren't sufficient enough to doom the Terra Nova expedition, Scott commanded his men to collect and carry rock samples throughout the entire journey to and back from the

South Pole. It was unnecessary weight added to the unexpected, absurdly heavy burden they already bore.

At the end of it all, Scott and the last remaining expedition member froze to death in their tent on March 29, 1912.

They were just eleven miles from a waypoint containing everything necessary for their survival.

THE JESTER AND THE PRINCE

"You know, things can go wrong just about anytime," Gene said. "And when you're so close to the final prize, it's particularly tough. But the important thing is making the effort. To go up there, and to follow your dreams. Keep on truckin' everybody."

When Robert Rodgers first learned of his brother Gene's plans to join the Team Everest '03 expedition, he did a very uncharacteristic thing. Though Robert (according to Gene) hadn't camped a day in his life, he decided he wanted to accompany Gene to base camp. Over the past nine years, they'd lost touch with one another. Robert looked forward to reconnecting with his brother, to sharing the latest of Gene's many adventures.

Things weren't easy in the beginning. Robert suffered from severe depression and crippling anxiety. In the past he was incapable of leaving his house, sometimes for months at a time. On this trip, he would intentionally leave all of his medication behind; he wanted to experience the real emotion of the journey. It flooded over him during the early days. Gene's seemingly inexhaustible patience would be put to the test.

Over time, Robert found his place on the team. He was the one responsible for making the others laugh. As he adjusted to life without the numbing-down effect of the medications he once took, he found his inner voice as well. It was that of the cartoon ogre Shrek.

Many times during the days and nights, Robert would break into character. Andy was quick to spin the camera Robert's way whenever he did because he knew something hilarious was likely to follow.

On the evening the team reached Gorakshep, however, Robert's voice would not be playful.

Gene became restless hours after settling into their tent. The first signs of danger came in the form of his intermittent moaning. Robert sat awake and alert next to him and observed the escalation, a look of growing concern on his face.

In the hours that followed, it became evident that Gene's condition was worsening. He was clearly in excruciating pain. Robert shined a flashlight on his brother as he asked him where the pain was originating. Gene slowly looked down at his stomach, which appeared as a balloon that had been inflated dangerously close to its bursting point.

Robert's voice bellowed loudly across camp. He called out for the doctor, and soon for Gary. He first knew that it had become a life-or-death situation when Gene began coughing up blood. He tried to take comfort in the knowledge that he'd be there for Gene when he passed away, that Gene was in Everest ... that he'd followed his dream until the very end.

They'd come within 300 feet of reaching base camp, and they could go no further. A rescue helicopter soon arrived as Robert bid farewell to the TE '03 team. Gary wrapped Robert in a giant one-armed bear hug. After letting go he began to pace nervously around Gene as he was lifted out of his chair and onto a stretcher.

Before Gene was taken, Gary said goodbye to him. His smile was one of reassurance; his words were of being reunited together again in Austin soon. His hand tightly clenched Gene's jacket. His vice-like grip betrayed his innermost feelings.

Gene told Gary: "If you run into trouble up there (Everest), give me a call." Gary stood silent, still holding the coat. Moments later he said: "I will. I promise."

The helicopter left a furious wind in its wake. The team had lost its jester and its prince.

The effects of altitude had begun to take their toll on the team many days before Gene's departure. Dinesh now stopped to recuperate every twenty feet, considerably slowing his already cautious pace. They all breathed in a belabored manner.

The team had reached 17,200 feet on the day Gene was evacuated. Hours after the helicopter, Lakpa Dorje Sherpa made his way back down the mountain toward lower ground. The altitude had claimed another member.

That evening the expedition's physician, Dr. Janis Tupesis, spoke to the team about Gene. He explained that Gene's intestines had rotated on themselves. The twisting caused a strangulation effect. All blood flow was cut off. It was as if he'd had a heart attack in his intestines.

Afterward, Andy shared the video message Gene had asked him to tape for the team before he left them.

It ended with this: "Keep on truckin.'"

SEVEN

CLARITY

MAKE

Be honest with those who are important to you

OTHERS

Embrace diversity. Accept those who are different from you. Make them welcome in your presence.

GREATER

Even the ghastliest of things can be overcome easily once the decision is made to do so

I n the spring of 2001, I trekked to Everest Base Camp as part of an international team that would attempt the world's highest mountain. Two months later, after a drunken return journey back to the US, I had no summit but had every excuse imaginable and reasons no one would dare question. I knew I hadn't prepared and the mountains hold little back for a bluff. Although I held my head high at the homecoming reception in Austin, TX, inside I was broken again. Still searching for some identity, I'd fallen prey to my own illusions of misguided grandeur and becoming an Everest Summiteer had eluded me.

—Gary Guller on his 2001 Everest summit attempt

UM SINCERO PRESENTE

The night was full of good music, of great company, of two people appreciating each other. She'd bought him a gift at the end of the night. The conversation it started played out over days.

Their talks would bring her back across many years of Gary's life. It would bring them closer, becoming the bridge over a growing chasm between them.

One brought into existence by extreme behaviors.

As he talked with her, their conversation carried him places too – through the dark years, over broken promises and through failed relationships, across the distancing from others that often became the next run or the further climb.

Caring for someone can only take a person to the edge a finite number of times before that care surrenders to the eventualities that a destructive force brings. Then the caring dissipates, creating distance in its wake.

At the end of the weekend, they understood their walk together in a new and healthier way. The destructive force further quieted itself. The edge began to disappear in the face of understanding and compassionate commitment.

He'd held up the white linen shirt she'd bought him in a way that showcased it to others. It was the first long sleeve shirt he'd considered wearing since the accident.

And that's when their relationship began.

LINES OF WHITE

The first word reflexively conjures a shortlist of names. Kurt Cobain, Janis Joplin, River Phoenix. The next forms a different list. Robert Downey Jr., Robin Williams, Drew Barrymore.

The words are *addiction* and *recovery*.

If we're not careful, we romanticize them into Hollywood-influenced images of street corners and pushers, of Nick Cage leaving Las Vegas, of Sinatra torn between his heroin addiction, his wheelchair-bound wife, and his true love, Molly.

Addiction defines the relationship between a person and the thing they can't let go of at any cost. Its easy association forms in liquor stores and with needles, in pipes and with pills, in lines of white and with hospital beds. Eventually it ends in jails or city morgues.

It's the club that has only one price for membership. *Give up everything.* Admission at the door covers more than just drugs or alcohol. Between the extreme edges of the addiction spectrum is a vast plane of grey. In the grey is a soft space that hosts a diverse array of behaviors on its grounds, for addiction has multiple forms and many faces. They're all admitted once the doorman gets paid.

On its destructive face it wears the mask of substance abuse for sure, but there are others. Some depict greed, some define the relentless pursuit of power, and still others outline the endless trail of excess. The masks capture the essence of disconnected ego, of dispassionate decision making that benefits the few in a way that harms the many.

Jeffrey Skilling may not have started out with ill intent. When the quarterly numbers didn't align, he simply made a small choice. He took an accounting principle that was meant to be used by businesses buying and selling securities and applied it to all facets of Enron's revenue reporting.

And so began his ride down the slippery slope leading him to the path of destructive addictive behaviors. One small choice makes the next minor bad choice easier to make. This then leads to the next, eventually down a path of no return. One inevitably filled with blatantly wrong, unforgivably bad choices.

Though the masks are sometimes first worn in benign, even admirable or noble ways, the intent behind donning them twists them into something far more harmful.

Regardless of intent, the end game is the same. Flooding the pleasure center. Always leaving a path of destruction.

HOKEY-POKEY

The subject of their experiment chased its next high by always returning to corner A.

Electrodes had been surgically placed deep inside the brain of the animal they'd selected. Long wires connected these electrodes to an electrical stimulation unit. It would deliver current to the areas the electrodes had been placed under the conditions scientists Peter Milner and James Olds selected.

The brain doesn't contain pain receptors; therefore the low-load current they'd introduced would elicit a response far different from pain in the animal they'd chosen.

The rat was placed in a four-cornered maze. It was free to explore and discover all areas with no consequence. That is, all areas except corner A. There the wires delivered a mild current to the waiting electrodes.

And there the rat's initial high was experienced.

The first visit led to a second, then to a third. The rat continually returned to corner A until it reached the point of exhaustion. Only then did it stray from corner A in order to find a place to rest. No area other than corner A held its interest until it reached the mental state of overstimulation, a point where it had to rest.

Each day of the experiment produced a similar pattern. It moved away only to immediately return. The rat hokey-pokeyed in and out of corner A in near perpetual fashion.

In the extreme, days into the experiment, stimulation occurred as often as 2,000 times in a 24-hour period. It eventually had to stop when the rat showed signs of malnutrition but still sought out corner A rather than choosing to eat.

The exhausted rat was left to rest and recover. A new candidate replaced him.

Corner A again became the destination of choice.

Milner and Olds next changed things up. They stopped administering low-load stimulation in corner A; consequently, the new rat began to explore the box. Now the researchers delivered their reward to the willing recipient when it approached corner B.

The new rat modified its hokey-pokey dance to corner B.

Over time Milner and Olds learned that they could reroute the rat at will by simply changing the location that the stimulation occurred in: a lighter load when the rat turned in the direction they wanted it to, a stronger load when the rat got closer, then full tilt when it arrived.

The area of the brain that Milner and Olds targeted was not the one responsible for curiosity. Nor was it the one in charge of understanding spatial relationships or directional navigation.

It was the pleasure center located in the brain of the rat.

They expanded their study to prove that pleasures had hierarchies. A male rat, for example, would self-direct toward electrode stimulation rather than pay attention to the female rat in heat placed in its path. Female rats would even abandon their pups in pursuit of the stimulus.[38] The drive for pleasure would prove stronger than the instincts of reproduction and nurturing. Instincts that had been genetically hardwired over countless centuries fell easily away under the promise of pleasure-center stimulation.

Neuroscientist David J. Linden[39] would connect the findings of this and other studies to correlational behaviors of a unique set of individuals. The corner A-seeking animal, according to Linden, exhibited similar behavioral motivations as did most of the following: extreme athletes, entrepreneurs, CEOs, and other high-level leaders and figures of prominence (celebrities, etc.).

High performance, it seems, is the "corner A" of this select group.

He'd show that risk-taking and novelty-seeking behaviors trigger the release of dopamine (the brain's pleasure chemical) in a similar manner as the rats had experienced in their repetitive dance toward corner A.

Corner A (for the group that Linden identified) equaled the risk of the unknown. It represented the thrill of the new and undiscovered, and its eventual conquering.

Linden advanced the theory that those who set out in pursuit of great accomplishments often exhibit a different manifestation of the same behavior – that of the pleasure seeker.

By syllogistic extension, that of the addict.

CONCRETE

The doctor had visited Gary in the weeks that followed the Orizaba fall to explain his condition. There was no way in the world his arm would come back. It would always be a part of him that existed in perpetual sleep. It would remain unresponsive to his commands to awaken and move for the remainder of his life.

On that day the first layer was poured. It would harden, and then the process would be repeated, over and over again. The path it formed led from neurosurgeon to neurosurgeon. They all repeated the same words.

Never again will it awaken.

The memory still rolled across his mind at the vulnerable moments. The flash of falling. Jerry's face. His hospitalization. Jerry's death. The doctor's news.

Jerry's death.

More layers were poured.

These led across continents, to the next high – that of altitude or that of substance. Often of both.

Nothing was enough and the next layers were poured. They covered friends. They smothered relationships. For a time they buried him deep underneath.

His arm lay useless at his side. It knocked over drinks at the dinner table. It interrupted intimacies. It kept him from going upward.

It reminded him of the fall.

One day, buried deep in the layers of protective concrete he'd poured upon himself, he made the decision to have it taken away.

AFOOT

During his 1999 trial Robert Downey, Jr. said: "It's like I have a loaded gun in my mouth and my finger is on the trigger, and I like the taste of gunmetal."

The actor is a bright light that was very nearly extinguished by the unrelenting and destructive pull of addiction. We watched his rise to fame in *Less Than Zero*, followed by his rapid descent from the small screen in *Ally McBeal* to a crystal-meth-filled hotel room in Palm Springs.

We watched the arrest as it led to the eventual trial and sentencing – to the very lowest of points in his life.

And then one day it was behind him, relegated to a view in his life's rearview mirror. "I reached out for help and I ran with it," he said. "It's not that difficult to overcome these seemingly ghastly problems; what's hard is to decide to actually do it."

The silver screen presents an illusory world capable of seducing us into accepting nearly anything. We see ancient Sparta unfold before us in the movie *300*, and it defies reality that it was manufactured on a green screen in Montreal, Canada. It therefore becomes as real as the brilliantly scripted lines of its lead, Gerard Butler.

We watch an old Schwarzenegger movie and ask ourselves how it could've happened. How we could've suspended reality long enough to accept that no matter how many villains were firing on him with automatic weapons, he could dodge and weave through their bullet storm virtually unharmed – and eventually kill them all, each with one well-placed shot from his handgun. We bought it by the bucketload back then.

And now a new breed of action hero has emerged, one whose skills transcend acting. When we watch the fight sequences in new Sherlock Holmes movies, we aren't asked to accept the implausible or impossible. In real life Robert Downey Jr. has studied martial arts for nearly eight years.

His skills are very real.

His drug of choice today is the chemical byproduct that his brain releases as a result of his training in an ancient art. Its origin is in the 17th Century Shaolin Temples of Southern China. It is Wing Chun, an art centered on balance and peace, accompanied by the very real and beautifully lethal violence that's only presented when all other options are eliminated.

Addiction has multiple forms and many faces. In its positive form it takes the shape of a cleaner way of life, embodying healthier and more life-affirming choices.

Dr. William Glasser has identified the six criteria that define positive addiction behaviors. They are noncompetitive and can be done in an hour; they don't require a lot of mental effort to do it well; they can be done alone; they have spiritual, physical, or mental value; they improve physical and/or psychological well-being; and they can be done without summoning the internal critic within.[40]

Replacing the mask of destructive addiction with one of the many forms of positive addiction is the key to sustainable success and happiness.

To reclaiming a career.

And to saving a relationship.

THE BEACH

We all have scars and imperfections. Some are visible to the eyes of others. Some only we can see.

Gary had held it up to admire it. His eyes narrowed on its two sleeves. They fell in perfect symmetry on either side of the shirt's yolk.

Then he looked down at himself. The reaction was visceral. His emotion was raw.

Then the words poured out.

There were years of his life that he simply hid his injury from the world, and from himself. He'd perfected the art of disguising his missing arm by tucking the sleeve of his jacket into the side pocket. This created the illusion of him having placed his (nonexistent) left hand into a pocket.

The world didn't look so closely at him when he did this. He therefore wore a jacket everywhere and always.

Then he stood on stage and spoke to members of the Coalition of Texans with Disabilities and at once came to terms with the acceptance of his injury. As he looked out over the audience in attendance, he didn't see people wearing coats. None attempted to disguise who they were.

A tsunami of realizations followed as he stood exposed to his peers.

And he decided on that day that he'd stop wearing the coat. He'd stop hiding the thing that made him different from the world around him.

Let them stare.

There was a progression to this, just as there is with all decisions that eventually alter the course of a life. It begins in the small, brave steps we take. We pronounce to the world who we really are, what we really are. To our surprise the world doesn't always shriek in retreat. Then momentum begins to build as we enhance the risk and increase the audacity of our progress.

What were once jackets became short-sleeve Hawaiian print shirts. It surprised him to find that the shock and awe he expected at the sight of his empty sleeve just didn't often happen.

It provided him a false sense of hope that the world was looking past the thing that made him different, that it could no longer see the missing part of him he'd surrendered years before.

For Gary, walking through a crowd at the beach with his shirt off is still harder than it was getting to the top of the world. He tries not to notice, but eyes are upon him and it's hard to ignore.

He describes his visits to a new swimming pool as causing time to stop. Like the movie *Inception*, all around him freeze-frame with open jaws as they stare at his shirtless body and try to reconcile themselves with what's there before them – and what isn't.

He reminds himself that he's different since the accident, that he always will be. That his differences don't define him, his character does. At least most of the time.

He's usually a snowflake. On occasion he's an avalanche.

He knows that he's a work in progress and freely admits to it.

He'd stopped wearing long-sleeve shirts because the empty left sleeve hung on his body in a way that reminded him of his once unresponsive left arm as it hung lifeless from him, before he'd decided to have it removed.

And this reminded him of the fall, a memory that he'd hoped the taking of his arm would erase.

We all have scars and imperfections, ones we hope will one day be invisible to others.

And to ourselves.

They can be directed toward something more positive.

EIGHT

Maoists, Masks and Makalu

MAKE

The word no has real power.
Don't invoke it unless you have to.

OTHERS

There are times when the masks must come off

GREATER

The fates will change in an instant.
Find that instant and seize it.

Lentils (Dal)

1½ cups lentil (any kind)
4 to 5 cups of water (depends on preference of your
   consistency of liquid)
1/2 tsp. turmeric
1 tsp. garlic, minced
6 tbsp. clarified butter (ghee)
3/4 cup sliced onions
2 chiles (dried red chiles preferred)
Salt to taste

Plain Rice (Bhat)

2 cups rice (Basmati or long grain preferred)
4 cups (1 liter) water
1 tsp. butter (optional)

—Courtesy of Chef Guller

IN & OUT

The message at first didn't resonate. I dismissed it too soon, too
reflexively.

❖   ❖   ❖

As we approached the halfway point of the draft, Gary asked his good friend Anil to read our book and provide feedback. Anil is a brilliant man, himself a gifted writer and translator. It was truly an honor for him to agree to the request.

His recommendations were dead on, all immediately adopted.

Except one.

Anil asked why "goodness in, badness out" wasn't included in any of the stories. I knew this phrase from the documentary film of the climb, and I wasn't attracted to it. I decided to call Gary. Anil had been spot-on in all his other recommendations. Why had he seemingly missed the mark on this one?

I quickly learned that he hadn't.

In the film, the scene featuring "goodness in, badness out" involved a group of Sherpa surrounding Gary in a semi-circle. As was his daily discipline, Gary gave a morning talk on what would be accomplished today, the dangers, etc.

At the end of the talk, he moved his right hand a short distance from his mouth. In a sweeping gesture meant to convey pulling something in, Gary said to the Sherpa: "Goodness in."

Next he exhaled, and while doing so he performed a gesture opposite to the other. Now he expelled something from his mouth.

"Badness out."

I'd soon learn that there was a far larger and more provocative story behind this simple phrase.

DIDDLE

Do we face our day as a prince or princess – or as a pauper?

The day begins with the unwelcome sound of an alarm clock. Startled, we knock over our glass of nighttime water. It spills across the book we read just before closing our eyes the night before.

The day goes on.

Mr. Coffee has once again clogged with grounds. There's a puddle of brown across the countertop, dripping onto the floor.

The puddle gets cleaned, but remnants remain. They cling to the base of the coffee cup and inevitably drip onto the clean white work shirt.

Shirts are changed. Cars are started. On to the morning commute we go.

We know with certainty that the mishaps that occurred before we left home were just coincidental. Happenstance.

And then we catch a red light. And then another red light, one after the other. Then the cars in front and beside us dance their car-blocking ballet together, and we're stuck behind them with no chance of passing.

And next we're late for work.

Now we're not so sure it's coincidence. We'll hesitate before admitting it out loud, but a part of us imagines there's a person somewhere who's responsible for all the morning's mayhem.

A person who has decided to diddle on our day.

THE DANCE

The last time Gary had passed through the region, he'd made a mental note not to return. Nature had made this route quite dangerous. It was replete with steep ascents, rockslides, and very technical descents.

And of course there was the local mafia boss to deal with. There was also a civil war to consider, and the fact that the route passed directly through one of the warring faction's strongholds.

It was October, 2002, smack dab in the middle of a war.

Here was the edge. Others took a step back. In went Guller.

It should be said here, before the rest of the story unfolds, that calculated risk taking and brinksmanship are always combined with careful consideration for the safety of the expedition members. Gary takes his responsibility for the others quite seriously. Sacredly, in fact.

But when that safety won't be compromised? Well, interesting things can happen.

I digress.

The journey will play out across three high-altitude passes: Sherpni Col, West Col (Baruntse Camp 1), and Amphu Laptsa Pass. The eventual end is Makalu Base Camp.

There were hints of what was to come earlier in the journey. A Maoist soldier was seen snooping around their camp the previous day, learning about their route, where they'd be next.

The day of the incident involving a kerosene lamp, some bombs, and Gary began when they marched into a small village that was at that time a Maoist stronghold.

The first moments played out in near slow motion. Gary and his team entered the village. Next to a teahouse were soldiers, young but hardened. They were wearing cammo outfits like Rambo; their automatic weapons leaned against the wall. Together they were doing jumping jacks.

Not one soldier was in synch with any other.

Gary tilted his head slightly, considering a smile. It was like he was watching a Maoist version of the movie *Stripes*. Except for this: Bill Murray was clowning. These guys were serious. And they had weapons.

The smile was a bad idea. It was a slippery slope guaranteed to lead to a full belly laugh.

The smile got put away.

The day progressed to night; the waiting started. Then the darkness came, the commandant behind it.

Gary had seen this dance before. The music had started; the dancers were limbering up before their performance began. The first movement would be the diversionary. It would soon transform into a mosh pit mangle.

It was a dance called the "Shakedown Samba," and the Maoist dancers had plans to add their own unique interpretation.

Next came the moments before the moment. The random sounds of the orchestra's warm-up exercises played in the background. The conductor cleared his throat. The dancers gave a last look to each other.

Then the dance began.

The commandant paid a visit to Gary's camp. He invited Gary and Nima Dawa to join him in a small thatch-roofed house nearby.

The invitation couldn't be declined. There were guns involved.

They entered and went up a set of stairs. They reached a ladder and climbed it. They were greeted by a small band of soldiers in the room.

The next steps of the dance began.

PEERS

In 2007 the *Journal of Consumer Research* conducted a study in which participants were given information on a new product that was (according to JCR) soon to be in stores. They were asked to form an opinion on the new product, then to record their opinion.

Once the consumer documented their impression of the product (either positive or negative), the story met with a twist. Researchers revealed the opinions of their peers to the participants on the product they'd just rated.

They found that the opinions of others, especially the negative ones, exerted a great deal of influence over the group. Consumers holding a positive impression of the product they'd reviewed could be swayed to a negative opinion. Sometimes easily swayed.

Further, they found that those holding a negative opinion became more vocal about their negativity when in a group setting.[41] This outspoken criticism was observed to domino across the team, feeding and fueling on itself.

John Cacioppo, PhD, of Ohio State University, was curious to better understand this seemingly overpowering weight of negativity. Using MRI technology, he recorded the effects that showing pictures evoking positive, negative, or neutral feelings had on a subject's cerebral cortex. He found that the brain reacted significantly stronger to the negative stimulus than to that deemed neutral or positive.

In a much simpler study, participants' brains were imaged in reaction to two words: one produced significant disruptions, the other didn't.

The words were no and yes.

◆   ◆   ◆

Negativity is an intoxicating drug. Break addictions to it by any means, and at all cost. Left alone it will overtake the sentiments of a group and often lead to devastating outcomes.

AND SO IT BEGINS

Nima Dawa and Gary took inventory of the motley crew before them. The soldiers wore side pistols. Some held more menacing weapons, odd, homemade pipe bombs held together (in some cases) by duct tape.

The soldiers embodied a potentially lethal set of characteristics: Young. Scared. Trying not to show it.

Clearly a bad combination.

With that it began. The long slow kiss.

The commandant placed a kerosene lantern on the table, resting inches from Gary's face. The shadow it cast reminded him of the movie *The Deer Hunter* and of the cheap interrogation tactic employed in an over-romanticized B-movie. Maybe a mix of the two.

The lamp made loud crackling noises. So did the Maoist commandant.

"Blah, blah, blah … our cause." "Blah, blah, blah … the Nepalese government." "Blah, blah, blah …." This was the foreplay.

Then the moment of intimacy arrived and the commandant showed his hand. He wanted money.

The dance of the Shakedown Samba was in full regale. It was both amusing and totally not amusing to Gary.

Nima Dawa was the interpreter, Gary was the target, and the commandant was the man in charge. Any doubt of this fact dissipated with a quick glance around the room, at the guns and the bombs.

The Maoist leader made his first demand; Nima translated it to Gary.

Gary knew that the Maoist didn't speak English.

Let the games begin.

THREE

The general who wins a battle makes many calculations in his temple ere the battle is fought. The general who loses the battle makes but few calculations beforehand. Thus do the many calculations lead to victory, and few calculations to defeat. How much more do no calculation at all pave the way to defeat! It is by attention to this point that I can see who is likely to win or lose.

— *The Art of War* by Sun Tzu

People's War tactics were so named by Mao Zedong. They're designed to leverage the advantages that a small revolutionary army offers.

It is a three-stage affair.

One: Occupy a remote area, one that can't easily be navigated. This levels the playing field against a larger opponent.

Two: Build and spread support from the locals through propaganda methods.

Three: Encircle and capture small cities, then larger ones. Then seize power over the country.

Nepal was the Maoist's target.

It began on February 13, 1996, and would last a brutal six years.

During these years Nepal turned red.

Gary was now in the middle of it.

JEKYLL AND HYDE

The journey toward great discovery and the journey up the mountain follow a similar course. There are miles upon miles where a view of the end goal is hopelessly obscured. Then there are beautiful vistas that reveal themselves at certain points along the path.

There are rockslides. There are stumbles. Then there's a Summit one day after the many miles.

My brother had boiled down his theory to its irreducible minimum. What decreases blood clotting and inflammation must also both reduce the incident of stroke and help those who've suffered one to better recover.

This breakthrough had hidden itself in plain sight from many before him. Like most things in life, it only became obvious once pointed out. It's the beautiful view of the mountain that was once obscured, and now is crystal clear.

Aerobic exercise has always been advocated for all adults, including those with heart disease, diabetes, and advancing age. To this point it was never recommended for stroke survivors. For them, the window closed on their recovery (as well as their mobility and independence) within three to six months of the stroke event.

But should it?

That was the question that changed it all.

In the early days there was a theory. When stroke creates paralysis, it also creates a corresponding damage path in the brain. In the wake of this brain trauma the neural pathways that are required for messages related to movement suffer varied degrees of impairment.

If a message could be sent to a more primal part of the stroke sufferer's brain, one that resided "below" the stroke-affected areas, perhaps a person could repair the pathways above and learn to walk again.

Promising studies performed years before found that cats with severed spinal cords were being taught to rhythmically step with their hind legs on a treadmill. Maybe the same could happen with human patients? Maybe treadmill walking could provide the necessary task repetition and progression needed to stimulate brain plasticity?

To test the theory, patients ranging from six months to twenty years post-stroke were selected. This was done to prove a point. And the point was resoundingly made when fitness levels, walking function, and economy of gait (gross motor efficiency) in the patient group all improved. Diabetes is a very common adjunct to stroke, and post-exercise the incidents of diabetes began to reverse in the patient group.

Success.

Today, the Maryland Exercise and Robotics Center of Excellence (MERCE)[42] is the first of its kind. My brother Richard, sister-in-law Charlene, and nephew Nate work there as part of the University of Maryland team. The focus of the MERCE center is the study of task-oriented exercise (primarily in stroke) and modular robotics (mostly for the lower extremities in stroke). Their randomized studies show that they can reverse prediabetes and non-insulin dependent diabetes and improve the neuromotor function of walking – even years after a stroke.

The vascular endothelium are the "Jekyll and Hyde cells" of the human body. When stimulated in one manner, they inflame and become clot promoting. When stimulated another way, they become health and clot protective.

Over the years their program would awaken the Jekyll cell in countless patients while keeping the Hyde persona disinterested.

KEROSENE

They wanted a "donation" toward their cause. A huge one. Too big.

"Tell him he's a goat and to stop bothering me," Gary said.

Nima cracked the Sherpa smile he's known for around the world. Then he translated Gary's words.

"Gary would like to know if you could speak more slowly."

"Now tell him he's a dog," Gary said. "And not a pretty one. Tell him that."

Nima: "Gary would like to know what we can do to help you."

There are times in one's life that the masks have to come off. Sitting in this dark room across from the commandant and the lads with the weapons was certainly one of them.

The air was hot, thick with kerosene and testosterone. "This was real negotiation," Gary would say to me later. "To this point no foreign traveler had ever been injured by the rebels. I surely didn't want my team members, Sherpa, and porters to be the first. Not at any cost."

◆   ◆   ◆

Enough was soon enough. It was time to bring this thing to closure. The glaring faces of the Maoist soldiers and the intense heat that radiated from the kerosene heater caused Gary to grow flush. He stood up and removed his coat, intending next to end it.

As Gary finished removing his down coat and lowered himself back into his seat, the rest of the room (except for Nima) froze, as if in a scene from the movie *Inception*. Gary recognized the looks; he'd seen them many times in public swimming pools he'd visited.

The down jacket had served its purpose. They'd just now noticed his arm.

Next, Mr. Hyde turned into Dr. Jekyll. The once destructive Maoist lost interest and the protective person inside him awakened.

The commandant explained to Nima (and Nima to Gary) that he'd like to significantly lower the "donation" amount. Further, he'd assure them safe passage through the region.

Later, Gary requested a handwritten note from the commandant that memorialized their agreement, along with a receipt. He would show them both to the next Maoist who attempted a shakedown.

The commandant willingly provided both, and the next day the team moved on.

Goodness in, badness out.

Suddenly I was very attracted to this concept. In a mere instant, negativity evaporates. Adversaries become friends. The mystery person stops diddling on the day. Mr. Hyde becomes Dr. Jekyll. In a moment bombs and guns are replaced with smiles and handshakes.

Goodness in, badness out.

A GLASS CASE

Several years ago I traveled to Finland on business. My host
picked me up at the Kokkola airport. We had important work to
do at the headquarters, but it would wait. First he would show me
Kokkola's prized trophy.

We traversed the inner harbor, then wheeled around a corner
and soon arrived at our destination: The English Park.

There he told me a story.

In the summer of 1854, 100 Finnish civilian volunteers assembled
next to two Russian infantry companies. On the evening of June
7th, the HMS Odin and HMS Vulture (that had been dispatched
by the British Royal Navy) arrived. Shallow water prevented the
large steam-paddle frigates from entering the harbor, so nine
paddle boats containing 197 men were dispatched to shore.

They came under the guise of negotiation; their true intent,
however, was to ransack the town. The citizens of Kokkola had
other plans, and after a 45-minute gun battle, the British Navy was
forced to retreat. Though a victory, one of the Finns' gunboats was
captured during the battle.

Its badly damaged remains are on display in The English Park
today. The CEO of HUR Fitness likes to bring all of his guests to
the English Park on their visit to Kokkola. He especially likes to
bring his many friends from England there.

I was reminded that day that there are some who simply don't
negotiate.

HOFFA

"I was born at night, but I wasn't born last night." *Here we go again,* thought Gary.

The Makalu region is notorious for its strong-arm tactics with regard to the use of its locals as porters. When passing through you will use the local porters, and you will pay them according to the fees that the local mafia man sets before you.

It's all decided in the village. There came a point in the trip where the porters that Gary and Nima brought weren't allowed to go any further. This left just the Sherpa, Gary, the client, and the Makalu mobsters – that is to say, the Makalu porters.

The commandant had settled his fee and so had the village mafia man. Five days later the opportunistic Makalu mobsters decided they wanted more money. They told Gary they were tripling their fee.

Guess who was a goat now.

Not Gary. Not Nima.

This wasn't what they'd agreed to. The two friends walked away from the negotiation, talked things over, then returned. Next they summarily dismissed the Makalu mobsters. They'd not be held ransom. Nima and Gary had agreed they'd carry their supplies themselves before they'd acquiesce to the opportunistic demands.

And that's exactly what they did.

Just past base camp proper, the "giant black one" came into view. At 27,825 feet Makalu is the world's fifth highest mountain. Despite the hardships, twists, and turns, it was now within reach.

Meanwhile, Gary had arranged a little surprise for the Sherpa. It waited for them at 18,000 feet. And it wasn't Dahl Baht.

Dal Bhat Preparation

Rice:

1. Wash rice and soak for 5 minutes.

2. Boil the rice over medium heat for about 10-15 minutes. Stir once thoroughly. Add butter to give taste to the rice and also to make it soft and fluffy.

3. Turn the heat to low and cook, covered, for 5 more minutes.

Lentils (see page 128 for ingredients):

1. Wash lentils and soak for 10 minutes.

2. Remove anything that floats on the surface and then drain extra water.

3. Add drained lentils to fresh water, then bring the new mixture to boil again. Add all spices.

4. Reduce heat and simmer, covered, for 20-30 minutes until lentils are soft and the consistency is similar to that of porridge.

5. In a small pan, heat the remaining butter and fry onions, chiles, and garlic.

6. Stir this mixture into the lentils. Serve with rice.

NINE

Cho La

MAKE

Have fun wherever possible

OTHERS

Stay focused. Keep moving.

GREATER

Commitment sometimes requires blind faith

When we finally get down to something that the individual really wants to do, I will say to them: You do that, and forget the money. Because if you say that getting the money is the most important thing, you will spend your life completely wasting your time. You'll be doing things you don't like doing in order to go on living – that is, to keep on doing things you don't like doing. Which is stupid. Better to have a short life that is full of what you like doing, than a long life spent in a miserable way.

—Narrative of "What if Money Was No Object?" video,
produced by Tragedy and Hope Communications

TEETH

It was Halloween, 2002. The holiday isn't usually celebrated in Nepal, but it would be celebrated that night. Gary had arranged something special for the Sherpa when they reached the 18,000-foot mark and formed the evening's camp.

They'd faced the rigors of the trail, armed Maoists had made hostages of them, and they'd carried unanticipated loads after the Makalu Mobsters were dismissed.

And they'd done it all (mostly) with smiles on their faces.

The Sherpa had earned a treat. Gary would see to it.

But first they'd have dinner. This dish, like Dahl Baht, was one of Gary's favorites.

Sherpa pizza.

"I describe the very interesting and unique dish developed out of sheer joy to others whilst away from their home 'Sherpa Pizza.' A mountain of a dish unlike anything you've ever seen. Cooked on kerosene burners that resemble a small rocket, with little or no control over the dispersing of heat. Crust that is thin in places and thick in others. Uncooked and burnt all at the same time. Endless toppings, primarily veggies, with a ketchup-based sauce. Funny really, in my experience it always resembles a mountain. The inside is not cooked thoroughly, the outer is usually slipping like minor pizza avalanches, and the cheese is melted, but randomly. Before it reaches your mouth, you'll wear part of it on your lap or your shirt, and you'll wonder if it will make it to the taste buds. It does, barely. Sherpa pizza. Who would've guessed that it tastes really good."

—GG, 3/30/13

With dinner complete, it was now time for their surprise.

One by one, each item was lifted from its hiding place. Vampire teeth. Fake blood. Halloween makeup. Treats.

"The Sherpa quickly figured out how to play tricks on each other after I explained the meaning of the holiday to them," Gary said.

Good food and good fun always matter to Gary. He'd learned their value many years before.

NO REUNION

A group of nine rich and powerful men met together at an upscale hotel in Chicago in 1923.

Those present were: Charles Schwab,[43] President of Bethlehem Steel; Samuel Insull, President of Edison General Electric; Howard Hobson, President of the Associated Gas and Electric System; Arthur Cutten, a highly successful wheat speculator; Richard Whitney, President of the New York Stock Exchange; Albert Fall, a member of President Hoover's cabinet; Jesse Livermore, a high-power Wall Street investor; Ivan Krueger, entrepreneur and financier; and Leon Fraser, President of First National Bank.

It's not known exactly what was discussed at their meeting, nor will it likely ever be. What is known is the unraveling effect that occurred in each of their lives afterward.

Fast forward twenty-five years.

Charles Schwab is penniless and has filed for bankruptcy protection. Samuel Insull and Arthur Cutten have lost every cent of their respective fortunes; both are penniless. Howard Hobson spends five years in prison on mail fraud charges and on his release suffers a nervous breakdown and is institutionalized. Richard Whitney is released from prison after his conviction on grand larceny charges. Albert Fall is pardoned after his conviction for accepting a $100,000 bribe. Ivan Krueger's company loses more than $250 million and becomes defunct; he and Leon Fraser both eventually take their own lives.

As for Jesse Livermore, he'd committed suicide eight years prior. After visiting a New York bar and having just two drinks, Livermore walked into the coatroom, sat down on a stool, and shot himself in the head.

It was seven days after Thanksgiving, 1940.

If any good came from their collective tragic ends, it's in the knowledge their story leaves us with. The mighty can fall; the powerful can lose it all. Monetary wealth is an illusion.

Good friends always matter to Gary. Money comes and goes. People and the moments shared with them are the lasting riches.

PEEPS

At 10 a.m. on Easter morning my phone rang.

It was a friend of Gary's named Marv Weidner, and he had stories to tell. It was great timing actually. He'd save me from eating the box of stale Peeps I'd bought myself at Target the day before.

We exchanged pleasantries, shared our backgrounds.

Then he began.

Twelve years prior, Marv had decided to give himself a 50th birthday present: he would visit Nepal. After some searching he ran across a company called Arun Treks and Expeditions USA that specialized in excursions to Nepal. It was Gary's company. Marv decided to meet his future guide in person before inking the deal.

He flew from Iowa to Austin, Texas.

Minutes into their first meeting, Marv noticed that an arm was missing. As Gary told him the story of Orizaba, it became very clear: Gary had faced the worst of possible climbing outcomes, yet here he was.

Still climbing.

He knew then that Gary was the real deal, and he liked that. It inspired his trust. He decided then and there that he'd spend his birthday with Gary.

To follow is a story of deep snow and sherpani catfights, of yak dung and near death. Of a marriage proposal and of violent illness. Of miracle seeds and size twelve shoes. Of songs from South Korea and of Dahl Baht.

Of raw deathbed honesty ... and the lifelong friendship that formed in the wake of it all.

The Peeps are in my garbage can. Handwritten notes from my conversation with Marv rest on a nearby table. Alongside them are the printed pages of an email Gary sent describing the events that follow. I'll go back and forth between the two looking for events in one that the other failed to mention.

I'm surrounded by coffee, water, Pacifica Clara, and the leftovers of a delicious meal my chef friend brought me two days prior.

Loreena McKennitt is playing in the background.

The stage is set to tell this story.

SNOWBALLS

Marv had asked Gary to orchestrate a trek through the Khumbu valley for him. Amidst the hiking and climbing he wanted to experience real Sherpa life firsthand.

Gary would deliver.

Marv was an experienced climber in his own right. As such he understood (having climbed 22 of Colorado's 14,000-foot peaks) the important considerations necessitated at altitude. He first noticed how immediately tuned in to altitude acclimatization Gary was.

He'd made a good choice in leaders.

Ghokyo Ri sits atop a peak in the Khumbu region of the Himalayas. It's located very near the largest glacier in Nepal. In Ghokyo Ri proper, there are a handful of stone houses, and Gary's friend occupies one of them.

They stayed the night in that house, and in the morning they repaid the Sherpa for his kindness by tidying up his front yard. This can mean different things in different countries. In America, for example, it may entail raking leaves or mowing lawns.

In Nepal it often means shoveling yak dung.

Gary and Marv started their work in opposite corners of the yard from the Sherpa and porters that accompanied them. They hadn't accomplished much when it all began.

Marv recalls a slight sensation of something splatting on his face, accompanied by the sound of something larger whizzing past his ear.

Then laughter.

Gary was throwing yak dung at him, and so began the first yak-dung fight of Marv's life.

Marv would learn that a yak-dung fight had many similarities to a snowball fight. You'd hide in the same ways. You'd giggle maniacally after hitting your opponent.

There were, however, obvious differences. The biggest was this: what they flung at each other was dark brown.

The second biggest: it had odor.

KISSES

Having cleaned up after the dung-fight, they said their goodbyes and again took to the trail. They went on through the day and eventually to their next stop; their resting point before the trek to Cho La began.

Gary had made arrangements for them to stay that evening with a female friend who lived in the town of Tagnag. Tagnag, at 15,420 feet, had just three occupied residences at the time. Two belonged to local yak herders; the third was a teahouse.

They'd arrived with hopes of finding a warm fire, Sherpa tea, and perhaps some potato pancakes awaiting them.

They found none of these things. Controversy had apparently erupted among two-thirds of Tagnag's citizenry prior to their arrival.

"I later learned that my friend had been kissing one of the yak herders. The yak herder's wife had appeared and she was angry. Soon a catfight broke out. The mountain police eventually carted them all down to the nearest local jail house."

—GG on the yak-herder kissing incident, 3/31/13

They'd learn in the morning that the participants of this Sherpa love triangle would stand in front of a judge in Namche Bazaar and the injured party would receive some form of reparation from the other. Likely the guilty one would be made to give the "injured party" a goat or a yak.

Regardless, tonight they needed a place to stay and there was only one option: a yak hut. A smelly 10x10 shack with just enough room for a few pieces of "furniture" and a small twig fire.

Within the hut they made themselves comfortable, seated atop sacks of potatoes.

Gary had stoked the twig fire just enough to make tea and to boil some thin instant noodles that would become their dinner. The smoke hung at three feet off the floor, making it impossible to sit all the way up.

After dinner they would go to sleep, and the next day Marv would awaken a 50-year-old, now living in the 14th Century.

GO CHINA

The birthday morning began in an interesting way.

From the other cot Gary watched Marv take a rather big stretch. At the end of it, Marv's hand landed smack in the middle of a wet slab of dung that barely clung to the wall. It was the wall's mortar, and it was obviously fresh.

Happy 50th Marv, and welcome to the 14th Century ... and to Sherpa country.

"Another 15 or so days followed with perhaps some of the greatest trekking I have ever experienced. We encountered nearly six feet of snow on the passes, the gathering of expeditions at Everest Base Camp, many a Sherpa tea, and copious of amounts of Sherpa laughter, Chaang, and outstanding hospitality. This is what Marv had signed up for. Sherpa house to Sherpa house, nearly a month of nonstop Sherpa indulgence.

We assisted with fertilization of the fields; we overcame the high altitude, the cold, and the smoke-filled kitchens of some of my dearest friends."

—GG, on Cho La, 3/31/13

Marv would provide me a few additional specifics that the ever-humble Mr. Guller had omitted.

Sometimes at this time of year, the trek across the Everest valley to Cho La was dry. Other times it simply wasn't. The march across it is described by some as "five days of hell."[44] Others warn: "While usually not technical in nature, the Cho La has been the scene of some very close calls due to falls in icy conditions, avalanches, and poor visibility."[45]

Today it was nothing but ice, rock, and snow. And pure danger. Marv had roped the Tetons; it was nothing compared to this. They made up a saying that day, and they used it quite often during the harrowing four-hour ascent.

"Go China."

It meant this: if they fell, their fall wouldn't stop.

Until they reached China.

The way up and through was a very steep climb. Marv would describe it to me as the closest he came in his life to falling to his death.

Above, Phorba Sherpa dug handholds and footfalls into the ice for him with his ice axe.

Every once in a while Marv would look down to check his footing. Each time he saw the same thing: Gary's size 12's placed just behind his, ensuring that he wouldn't slip.

He would say later about this experience that Gary had saved his life, literally the entire way up.

NANOQ

My second trip to Finland happened in the summer. That year I was an invited presenter to my host company's international sales and distribution team meeting.

When the workday reached its end, we piled into a chartered bus. Next stop was Nanoq, a famous museum in Jakobstad, Finland, dedicated to arctic cultures and polar expeditions.

There we were regaled by stories of ancient Norsemen and recent Finnish heroes. We enjoyed a wonderful banquet together, seated at a table that was many times older than even the oldest person at the table.

Then it began.

It's a Finnish custom that whenever a group of people from other countries gathers together for dinner, each person at the table has to sing a song from his native land.

The award for the most animated easily went to the Brits. Their song involved them standing on their chairs and spinning in circles while they sang. This was incredible to watch as the evening involved a lot of wine and other such things.

The Finns, led by my friend Anssi, stood together and acted out their song about a drunken man who climbs out the window and runs for his life when the husband unexpectedly returns home. Since the running man didn't know that his bed-partner was married, there were animated (and hilarious) looks of shock and surprise throughout each verse.

When it came to my turn I did everything I could to get out of it. I even resorted to hiding outside. The group was having none of it.

Eventually I sang. "Johnny Tarr" by Gaelic Storm to be exact.

When the night was over there were no longer Brits, Finns, or Americans. Nor were there Germans, Russians, or Italians. There were only friends.

I thought about Nanoq as Marv continued his story.

ALWAYS BOIL

At the conclusion of a white-knuckled four-hour climb, they reached the top of Cho La.

There they were greeted by a near whiteout blizzard.

They had quite a distance to go to reach their next destination. For more than three hours they "post-holed" through three-foot high snow. When they arrived at their destination, they found the teahouse closed.

It was still Marv's birthday.

They had no other option than to continue trekking. Gary warned Marv that it would be a long haul.

Seven hours later they arrived at another teahouse. Gary's friend Pemba owned this one and it was open.

There, fifteen-plus hours after sticking his hand in fresh yak dung, Marv entered the last phase of his birthday celebration.

A team from South Korea was staying in this rather large teahouse at the time that Gary and Marv arrived. They'd just completed their Everest summit. It was time for festivities.

The night was filled with songs from South Korea, stories of the climb, rice wine, and chaang.

Music and stories.

◆   ◆   ◆

Marv's birthday marathon ended at 3 a.m. Or so.

The next morning they said goodbye to their new friends and set out for Namche Bazaar. Along the way they stopped at a small teahouse with two large yaks living on the ground floor.

And in that teahouse a chain of events were set in motion that very nearly claimed Marv's life.

Gary's written more in his email. At times a deep, philosophical thought weaves through his narrative. As I've come to know through our collaboration, when this happens it's never a random neural misfire; it's Gary's mind reconciling the lesson learned from an experience he's about to share.

"Why does it seem sometimes that when all is going so smooth, we question the seamlessness? A great friend, an India scholar, once told me: "Action cannot happen unless the thought is created. Positive or Negative, they both run parallel."

Gary then cites one of his favorite quotes…

"What you do makes you better at what you think. What you think makes you more effective at what you do.

Take action, after thinking through the consequences that are likely to come from that action. Put some thought into what you intend to do, and then get busy doing it.

Express your best, most authentic thoughts with your actions. Focus and empower your actions with your thoughts.

Balance the informed intelligence of your thoughts with the practical effectiveness of your actions. Thought without action is not worth much, and action without thought can be even worse.

True excellence results from the synergy of thought and action. Both are vitally necessary, and neither one is very beneficial without the other.

Consider, question, observe, evaluate, intend, plan, and then do. Think about what you're doing, and then get busy doing what you think."

—Ralph Marston

Gary then continues …

Nearing the end of our trek, the weather turned sour and we landed in the village of Khumjung. The village is home to the Hillary School, opened in 1961 with the hard work of Sir Edmund Hillary and the Himalayan Trust. And of course it contains a famous relic within, the Yeti Skull.

We decided to relax with Sherpa friends for a couple of days, have a small party for Marv, and dry our smelly wet clothes and enjoy the remaining couple of days prior to our trek to Lukla to catch our short flight back to Kathmandu.

Then it all went horribly wrong …

Marv's health had turned for the worse. He had been strong for the entire trek, acclimatized extremely well with not one stomach disorder, and thoroughly enjoyed all of the fabulous Sherpa cuisine that was thrown at him.

We were only a day away from Lukla when my friend suddenly couldn't move.

Marv tells the next part of the story to me.

ESQUERDA, DERECHA

At 28,840, the Hillary Step is the last major obstacle Gary will encounter before reaching the summit of Everest. It is a perpendicular upright spur of ice and snow that's approximately 40 feet in height. It stands 180 feet from Everest's peak.

The Hillary Step is navigated with the use of ropes fixed to the mountain. Their presence shouldn't imply that the area is easily navigable, however, for the Step doesn't offer walk-in-the-park passage.

In May 2012, the worst disaster on Everest in sixteen years occurred there.[46]

Below the Hillary Step, in the Lhotse Pass area, 150 climbers stood in a single line waiting for their turn to ascend the Step.

Temperatures reached a dangerous 20°C.

Wait times exceeded three hours.

The picture taken before events turned dire resembled the line one might see awaiting the Indiana Jones ride at Disneyland on a very busy day, except that it forms at life-ending altitude on a steep incline covered in ice and snow.

Cold, exhaustion, and the burning up of all remaining oxygen are imminent threats and they take their toll. At the end of it all, climbers from South Korea, China, Germany, and Canada would surrender their lives to Everest there (later to be joined by five others on the descent).

On the day of his summit Gary changed oxygen bottles just before reaching the Cornice Traverse, as is traditionally done. Many an expedition had been forced to make a difficult decision there: to abandon their summit efforts (so close to the end) due to an impending storm or the lateness of the day.

The weather and the day had both decided to cooperate with Gary's climb.

The Cornice Traverse is a knife-edged ridge of snow plastered on the intermittent rock that lies just before the Hillary Step is reached. It's the most exposed section of the climb. A wrong step to the right rewards the climber with a 10,000-foot fall down the Kangshung Face. To the left waits an 8,000-foot fall down the Southwest Face.

He'll make it through, then face a remarkable choice.

JUST RIGHT

Another memory hits me.

My daughter Bridget was emphatic about her birthday wishes. On her 10th birthday, she wanted to go rock climbing.

I organized the expedition.

We arrived; we tried on shoes. We were briefed; we were roped in. Above me stood a 15-foot wall.

Though I'd been climbing a time or two before, I was by no means an expert. I decided early on in the ascent to use whatever handholds and footholds I encountered, rather than following the color-coded sequences.

Just above the ten-foot mark I lost momentum. I'd been pulling myself up with the strength of both hands and arms, balanced with the requisite perching and foot balance. I was tired. I'd run out of next moves.

I would slowly lower myself down and step out of my safety harness.

Bridget greeted me there with a high five.

I remind myself today that I was 28,825 feet below the height that Gary would stand, looking up at Hillary Step.

For him, there was no briefing to be done other than the following. "You will climb these 40 feet without the benefit of the use of your left arm. You will rely heavily on your crampons, your foot balance, and the strength of your right arm. No one missing an arm has ever done this before you, so no one can advise you how (or if) it can be done. Good luck."

At the base of the Hillary Step, Gary pulled himself up slightly. He then dug one crampon into the ice. He followed it with the next, and then began to move.

Looking down between his legs, he saw an unsurvivable fall; above him an unimaginable challenge. Thoughts of Orizaba were dismissed by necessity, replaced simply by this:

"I'll go up, or I'll fall to my death. There is no other option."

No pause in between thought and action.

Upward he went.

PONGMORE

Hydration is an absolute requirement to sustain life at altitude, but it can threaten life as well. The water Marv drank at the last teahouse hadn't been boiled, and it was rife with contagions. Many days later, after the crisis was over, they'd theorize about possible yak contamination. To this day they're not completely sure of the cause of Marv's illness, only of its life-or-death severity.

There are unmistakable moments in life when things are undeniably wrong.

The mild pains Marv felt advanced at speeds surpassing those driven by the wildest of drivers on the Autobahn. It became as though a knife was repeatedly stuck into his intestines. It was the day after his birthday when the vomiting began.

Marv lay in bed, violently retching at least once nearly every quarter-hour. After several hours, a weakened and scared Marv looked over at his friend and asked him a question few will ever need to ask another.

"Gary, am I dying?"

Marv chuckled as he told me Gary's answer.
      "Man, I don't know."

In hindsight, Gary said, that was probably not exactly what Marv wanted to hear, but after barely a month together, 24-7, in a rather extreme environment, you learn very quickly the ability to cut through the crap and be brutally honest. I had never experienced this condition before; it was like he had eaten something poisonous by mistake. That did not make sense though; I was eating the exact same. Or maybe he had been bitten by something, but again that didn't make sense either. Me, my old Sherpa friend, his friends – we were all stumped.

After a couple of days, my Sherpa friend pulled me to the side and suggested that we try some "local" medicine. He was adamant that Marv was poisoned in some way or even perhaps that there was a "spell" placed on him by mistake. Only God knows.

My Sherpa friend explained this local medicine to me. He called it *Pongmore*. A small nut-like piece that resembled an almond, it was wrapped in a small paper napkin. He said there were two types: one that would cure you and one that could kill you. He described that if you were to put it in a bowl of water with some "sick" in the bowl, this nut-like substance would chase the sickness around and around the bowl until it disappeared.

Unfortunately, he was unsure of the variety he had. He thought it was of the "curing" variety but not one hundred percent sure.

Dilemma.

I decided to approach Marv and suggest we try the local medicine. I did explain to him that we were a little unsure of the variety. We were confident, but I offered no guarantee.

The choice would ultimately be his, but Marv did ask my opinion. I said, shit Marv, I'd go for it. You're nearing death's door at the moment; there's the slight risk that the variety is wrong, but hey, the upside has huge potential … your life.

Two days later, after more than a hundred extreme vomiting episodes, Marv sat up, looked at me, and smiled.

—Gary Guller on the Pongmore seed incident, 3/31/13

$150

There are no assurances of success or safe passage once we step out the doors of our homes in pursuit of the quest. All we can know with any degree of certainty is this: we'll each be a different person at journey's end.

Once we pass the threshold we become bound to the pursuit. Each step we take beyond that point dictates our expedition's success or failure.

Do we step in faith toward the bowl containing the Pongmore seed, or do we surrender to the inevitabilities that await us if we abandon the hope it holds because of the uncertainty it presents?

Do we stand at the base of the Hillary Step and choose the third option, to abandon the ascent none before us has ever made, or do we reach for the uncertainty that awaits us above while in clear view of the end that awaits us below?

Do we lead the largest team of persons with disabilities to ever reach Mt. Everest base camp, with extended plans to then summit Mt. Everest, or do we abandon these ideas as foolhardy?

Do we look boldly in the face of the New Normal and bravely make the changes necessary to champion its challenge, or do we quietly ignore the threat while comforted in our state of denial, one that comes complete with the belief that things will once again return to how they once were?

Such are the decisions faced by leaders in pursuit of that which is bigger than themselves.

Days after surviving his near-death illness, Marv sits on a small boulder at the edge of Namche Bazaar. There he'll remain for nearly half the day.

He replays scenes from the days and weeks before in his mind. The yak-dung fight, Gary's size twelve shoes stacked closely behind his.

His choice to see Nepal, and his decision to partake of the Pongmore seed.

Later in the day he leaves the small boulder. There is only one thought now: to reach a phone.

When he finds it, it's nearly the size of a Volkswagen. The phone call he'll next make won't be cheap, but it will be the most cherished $150 he ever spends.

He lifts the receiver to his ear, awaits someone in Kathmandu to broker the next connection, and then listens as the phone rings.

On the other end of the world it's 3 a.m. His (then) girlfriend Marty answers.

Before Nepal, Marv had "sworn off" marriage. It was understood between him and Marty that they'd be in a committed relationship, but no nuptials would ever follow.

While sitting on that small boulder in Namche, he'd come to a different place, a place he reached as the aggregate result of all his experiences with Gary. His call to Marty that day was to ask for her hand in marriage.

Thirteen years later he has no regrets. Nor does Marty.

It's human nature to sometimes downplay the positive in favor of the negative. The often irresistible draw of the negative pulls us in the direction of the remembrance of those we've hurt, and sometimes it blinds us to the realization of the many blessings we've given others.

The appreciation of Gene by the Sherpa, the many wheelies Matt sprung his chair into. The smile on Barry's face as he caught the Frisbee. The flag that hung atop the icefall with stars in the shape of a wheelchair.

Shannon Ardoin.

Marv and Marty.

Perhaps none of these things would've come to pass had Gary stopped climbing after the loss of his arm.

With regard to exceptional accomplishments, are they the result of an exceptional person meeting a challenge, or is it the challenge that brings out the exceptional nature of a person?

After asking myself, I realize that it's in fact both.

As I write the last words of this book, I realize how blessed I am to have had the opportunity to tell Gary's story, to learn from him about the beauty and majesty that is the mountain, to see the Sherpa culture through his eyes, and to meet the amazing people who joined him along the way.

And as I look back across the experience of completing this book, I realize a taste of what Marv must have felt while climbing Cho La. From the very first word through these final ones, Gary's size 12's have been just behind mine, ready to catch me if I stumbled, and ready to lead me to the summit.

There are times in our lives that define us. By their very nature they split our lives equally in half – into pre-event, and every day after.

How we handle those moments is often what defines us and gives true meaning and purpose to our lives.

Is climbing Everest or Cho Oyu really so different from our own everyday experience? In the obvious and extreme ways, yes.

Yet at points and times in our lives, we all inch across the traverse that holds danger to its left and right. We all stand at the base of our own Hillary Step, either feeling (or knowing) that something vital to its successful ascent is missing within us.

And then we choose to go on.

We survive our own fall and lie battered and broken at the bottom of it.

Then we choose to get back up, and it is the pure majesty of this choice that inspires others to reach greater heights themselves.

In this way, and in every decision along the way, we make others greater.

THANK YOU, MEA CULPA
AND THE FUTURE

I was born a Catholic, adopted at 10, had a Bar Mitzvah at 13, then lost my arm at 20. And I climbed Mt. Everest at 36.

There is so much to be appreciative for in my life. Most importantly, life itself. My journeys have taken me around the globe, across many countries, and to the very top of the world. I have also ventured to the bottom of hell. I struggle with addictions, desire, acceptance, and the dream. I never give up and I will continue to try – to be a better person. Whatever that dream or answer is for me – be it a mountaintop, a desert, cultures far away, or simply cooking Indian food for friends of like mind – I will always be searching for that answer.

For those who did not waver in their support of me, I thank you all from the bottom of my heart. You know exactly who you are. I achieved my blessings because of you. Honestly, I feel I do not warrant such loyalty, but you have stuck with me throughout this journey. A special thank you to my family. My mom, my father (Jeff), and my brothers and sister, you saved my life. I thank you a million times.

For those I have hurt along the way, I'm deeply sorry for my immaturity. There is no doubt in my mind that I am a "piece of work," but I do learn from my mistakes, and I will be accountable for my past behavior forever. Saying this, I do appreciate the time we spent together and all we enjoyed. I choose to focus on the wonderful experiences that transpired during our friendship.

I had a vision ten years ago, and it hasn't changed. It's about people having the choice to live the life they choose. It's about ability and freedom and the endless pursuit of happiness.

—Gary Guller

Gary enjoying the moment in Hawaii

REFERENCES

[1] Frater, Jamie. Listverse.com's *ultimate book of bizarre lists: fascinating facts and shocking trivia on movies, music, crime, celebrities, history and more*. Berkeley, CA: Ulysses Press, 2010.

[2] Drucker, Peter. "Management's New Paradigms." *Forbes*, October 12, 1998. http://www.forbes.com/forbes/ 1998/1005/6207152a.html (accessed November 9, 2012).

[3] Birkinshaw, Julian. "What Makes a Company Resilient? – BusinessWeek." *Businessweek* - Business News, Stock market & Financial Advice. http://www.businessweek.com/articles/ 2012-10-16/what-makes-a-company-resilient (accessed October 28, 2012).

[4] Watkins, Thayer. "The Rise and Fall of Enron." Powering Silicon Valley | San Jose State University. http://www.sjsu.edu/faculty/ watkins/enron.htm (accessed March 28, 2013).

[5] LaBier, Douglas. "The New Resilience." *Psychology Today*, April 5, 2010. http://www.psychologytoday.com/blog/the-new-resilience/201004/what-is-the-new-resilience (accessed November 1, 2012).

[6] Whitacre, Eric. "Eric Whitacre: Part of Something Larger Than Ourselves." Breaking News and Opinion on *The Huffington Post*. http://www.huffingtonpost.com/eric-whitacre/virtual-choir_b_2175526.html (accessed February 21, 2013).

7 Kouzes, James M., and Barry Z. Posner. *The Leadership Challenge.* 3rd ed. San Francisco: Jossey-Bass, 2002.

8 Gallo, Carmine. "7 Sure-Fire Ways Great Leaders Inspire People To Follow Them." *Forbes*, September 6, 2012. http://www.forbes.com/sites/carminegallo/2012/09/06/7-sure-fire-ways-great-leaders-inspire-people-to-follow-them/ (accessed September 17, 2012).

9 Wurtzel, Alan. *Good to Great to Gone: The Sixty Year Rise and Fall of Circuit City.* New York, NY: Diversion Books, 2012.

10 Alan Wurtzel (the author) held the top position at Circuit City from 1973 to 1986, and remained on the board until 2001.

11 Wurtzel, Alan. *Good to Great to Gone: The Sixty Year Rise and Fall of Circuit City.* New York, NY: Diversion Books, 2012, The Undisciplined Pursuit of More.

12 A *khata* is a traditional Tibetan offering scarf.

13 "High Altitude: What Happens to the Human Body in the 'Death Zone.'" *Summit Post*, January 7, 2008. http://www.summitpost.org/high-altitude-what-happens-to-the-human-body-in-the-death-zone/371306 (accessed November 23, 2012).

14 Maxwell, John C. *The 17 Indisputable Laws of Teamwork: Embrace Them and Empower Your Team.* Nashville: T. Nelson, 2001.

[15] Morrell, Margot, and Stephanie Capparell. *Shackleton's Way: Leadership Lessons from the Great Antarctic Explorer*. New York: Viking, 2001.

[16] The full story of Shackleton is told in an eloquent and riveting manner in the book Shackleton's Way. Morrell, M., and Capparell, S. (2001). *Shackleton's Way: Leadership Lessons from the Great Antarctic Explorer*. New York: Viking.

[17] Carr, Alan. *Positive Psychology: The Science of Happiness and Human Strengths*. Hove: Brunner-Routledge, 2004.

[18] Shill, Walt, John F. Engel, David Mann, and Oleg Scatteman. "Corporate agility: Six ways to make volatility your friend | Accenture Outlook." Accenture | Management Consulting, Technology and Outsourcing. http://www.accenture.com/us-en/outlook/Pages/outlook-journal-2012-corporate-agility-six-ways-to-make-volatility-your-friend.aspx (accessed February 23, 2013).

[19] Mipham, Sakyong. *Ruling Your World: Ancient Strategies for Modern Life*. New York, NY: Morgan Roads Books, 2005.

[20] Squires, Nick. "Italian art historians 'find 100 Caravaggio paintings' – Telegraph." Telegraph.co.uk - *Telegraph* online, Daily *Telegraph*, Sunday *Telegraph – Telegraph*. http://www.telegraph.co.uk/culture/art/art-news/9379713/Italian-art-historians-find-100-Caravaggio-paintings.html (accessed December 10, 2012).

21 Kington, Tom. "Secret stash of 100 'Caravaggio sketches' found in Milan castle | Art and design | The *Guardian*." Latest US news, world news, sport and comment from the *Guardian* | guardiannews.com | The *Guardian*. http://www.guardian.co.uk/artanddesign/2012/jul/05/caravaggio-discovery-milan-castle (accessed January 5, 2013).

22 Conwell, Russell H. *Acres of Diamonds*. Philadelphia: John D. Morris and Co., 1901.

23 Karmali, Naazneen. "Azim Premji Donates $2.3 Billion After Signing Giving Pledge." *Forbes*, February 23, 2013. http://www.forbes.com/sites/naazneenkarmali/2013/02/23/azim-premji-donates-2-3-billion-after-signing-giving-pledge/ (accessed February 26, 2013).

24 Self, Abigail, Jennifer Thomas, and Chris Randall. "Measuring National Well-Being: Life in the UK 2012." ONS Home. http://www.ons.gov.uk (accessed January 11, 2013).

25 Office of National Statistics UKEA and Blue Book, World Database of Happiness.

26 The US leads the world in obesity rates, followed closely by Mexico (30%), New Zealand (27%), and Australia (24%). In the Asian countries, the rates fall well below 5%; there is no data for Nepal. Source OECD.

27 Gallup-Healthways Well-Being Index.

[28] Pentland, Alex. "The New Science of Building Great Teams." *Harvard Business Review*, April 2012.

[29] Key Performance Indicators.

[30] Gallup Study: "Engaged Employees Inspire Company Innovation." Gallup Business Journal. http://businessjournal.gallup.com/content/24880/gallup-study-engaged-employees-inspire-company.aspx (accessed February 24, 2013).

[31] Denning, Steve. "Why Did IBM Survive?" *Forbes*, July 10, 2011. http://www.forbes.com/sites/stevedenning/2011/07/10/why-did-ibm-survive/ (accessed January 23, 2013).

[32] "Mahindra Reva seeks to co-imagine and co-create the Future of Mobility with the new 'Ask' Movement." Mahindra.com | Rise. http://www.mahindra.com/News/Press-Releases/1363000139 (accessed February 28, 2013).

[33] "Mahindra Reva seeks to co-imagine and co-create the Future of Mobility with the new 'Ask' Movement." Mahindra.com

[34] Morrell, Margot, and Stephanie Capparell. *Shackleton's Way: Leadership Lessons from the Great Antarctic Explorer*.

[35] "NOVA Online | Shackleton's Voyage of Endurance | Timeline 1914-1916 | PBS." PBS: Public Broadcasting Service. http://www.pbs.org/wgbh/nova/shackleton/1914/timeline.html (accessed February 5, 2013).

36 Cohen, Jennie. "Famous Expeditions That Fell Off the Map —
History in the Headlines." History.com — History Made Every
Day — American & World History. http://www.history.com/
news/famous-expeditions-that-fell-off-the-map (accessed
February 5, 2013).

37 Gonzalez, Robert. "10 Mistakes That Caused the Most
Punishing Nature Expedition in History." io9 - http://io9.com/
5874145/ten-deadly-mistakes-made-on-the-real-terra-nova-
expedition (accessed February 5, 2013).

38 Linden, David J. *The Compass of Pleasure: How Our Brains Make
Fatty Foods, Orgasm, Exercise, Marijuana, Generosity, Vodka,
Learning, and Gambling Feel So Good*. New York: Viking, 2011.

39 Linden, David J. *The Compass of Pleasure*.

40 Glasser, William. *Choice Theory: A New Psychology of Personal
Freedom*. New York: HarperCollins Publishers, 1998.

41 Adam Duhachek, Shuoyang Zhang, and Shanker Krishnan,
"Anticipated Group Interaction: Coping with Valence
Asymmetries in Attitude Shift." Journal of Consumer Research:
October 2007.

42 To learn more about the breakthrough treatment of stroke
taking place at the University of Maryland, visit http://
www.umm.edu/neurosciences/stroke.htm.

43 NOT the famed investor and namesake of his investment firm
Charles Schwab.

[44] Velder, Bianca. "Bianca Velder Creations: Chola Pass – part of the 5 days from hell." Bianca Velder Creations. N.p., n.d. Web. 1 Apr. 2013. http://biancavelder.blogspot.com/2012/10/chola-pass-part-of-5-days-from-hell.html.

[45] Reynolds, Kev. "Cho La at InsidrInfo.com | Online Cho La Pass guide with Cho La info and photos." Trekking at InsidrInfo.com | Online Trekking guide with Trekking info and photos. N.p., n.d. Web. 1 Apr. 2013. <http://trekking.insidrinfo.com/everest-trek/cho-la/.

[46] Wilkes, David. "The traffic jam at 30,000 feet: Chilling photo shows dozens of climbers trying to reach the summit of Mount Everest after four died when they became stuck in a bottleneck | Mail Online." Home | Mail Online. N.p., n.d. Web. 5 Apr. 2013. http://www.dailymail.co.uk/news/article-2151418/The-traffic-jam-30-000-feet-Chilling-photo-shows-dozens-climbers-trying-reach-summit-Mount-Everest-died-stuck-bottleneck.html.

ABOUT THE AUTHORS

GARY GULLER is both a world-renowned, record-setting mountaineer and professional motivational and inspirational speaker, celebrating 10 years of successful keynotes, trusted by the world's top corporations. In 2003, Gary was leader of the largest ever cross-disability group to reach Mt Everest Base Camp, at 17,500 feet. After setting this record, he went on to scale the peak, reaching the summit on May 23, 2003, and becoming the first person with one arm to summit Mt. Everest. Later the next year, Gary lead an expedition to the summit of the world's sixth highest mountain, Mt. Cho Oyu, located in Tibet.

In April 2010, Gary completed the grueling Marathon des Sables in Morocco. The MdS is a 6-day, 153-plus miles (250km) endurance race across the Sahara Desert – "The hardest stage race in the World" (CNN World News). Gary has gone on to become a trusted keynote speaker and personal executive coach.

On June 2, 2012, Gary successfully completed the Ironman 70.3 Kohala Coast, Hawaii – 1.2 mile swim, 56 mile bike, 13.2 mile run. Thank you all for the continued support.

Reach out to Gary and say hello at:
http://www.facebook.com/MakeOthersGreater

To learn more about Gary, or to inquire about a speaking engagement, visit www.garyguller.com
email: info@garyguller.com
or visit:
www.makeothersgreater.com
email: info@makeothersgreater.com

PHILLIP MACKO has had successful careers spanning four distinctly different industries: restaurant/hospitality, distribution, medical diagnostics, and music publishing. He has trained sales professionals from dozens of countries around the world in his travels and was an invited presenter at the World Congress of Physical Therapy. He's worked extensively in Finland, Germany, Canada, Brazil, Colombia, and (of course) the domestic US as a trainer and consultant. He is currently SVP of Sales at Megatrax Music and lives in San Diego, CA. He published his first book, *Think Your Age, Don't Act It* under the banner of Second Starters® Publishing (www.secondstarters.com).

You can reach Phil by leaving a message on the
Make Others Greater Facebook page at:
http://www.facebook.com/MakeOthersGreater
or visit:
www.makeothersgreater.com
email: info@makeothersgreater.com

The

MAKE OTHERS GREATER™

Facebook Project

To encourage and recognize the dynamic innovators, explorers, and everyday heroes who are making others greater in our current global community, we invite you to share your stories of those who lift others up so that more people can be inspired to do the same.

Once you've submitted your story, we will contact you for a more in-depth conversation, and over the next year we'll choose our favorite. We will offer a cash donation to the charity of your choice and in your name for the most enlightening stories.

Join the forum ... and the circle of love ... as we each strive to Make Others Greater.

www.facebook.com/MakeOthersGreater

67745830R00109

Made in the USA
San Bernardino, CA
27 January 2018